THE
National ‹SABR› Pastime

Pacific Ghosts: San Diego Baseball History

Edited by Cecilia M. Tan

 **Published by The Society for American Baseball Research**

THE NATIONAL PASTIME

Copyright © 2019 The Society for American Baseball Research

Editor: Cecilia Tan
Design and production: Lisa Hochstein
Cover design: Lisa Hochstein
Fact checker: Clifford Blau
Proofreader: Norman L. Macht

Front cover image: Detail from a 1945 PCL Padres program
Heading photo: San Diego Padres

ISBN
Print: 978-1-943816-83-5
E-book: 978-1-943816-82-8

Society for American Baseball Research, Inc.
Cronkite School at ASU
555 N. Central Ave. #416
Phoenix, AZ 85004

Phone: (602) 496–1460
Web: www.sabr.org

Contents

The Guide to Spalding

San Diego, 1900–15

Mark Souder

Albert Spalding lived an extraordinary life as one of baseball's most important figures. This article focuses on his San Diego years, during which he helped develop San Diego into the city it is today, as well as key connections in his early life that set up his grand finale.

THE ROCKFORD FILES

Rockford, Illinois, is an industrial city on the Rock River, 80 miles northwest of Chicago. Nineteenth-century baseball fans know it as the home of the Rockford Forest Citys of the National Association, which had a one-year life in that organization. Albert Spalding was born in Byron, 13 miles southwest of Rockford along the Rock River, on September 2, 1850. His father died when Albert was only 8 years old. Albert had already been sent to Rockford to live with his aunt. After his father's death, the rest of his family followed.[1]

Rockford established the most important connections for Spalding in business, baseball, and his personal life.

Albert Spalding learned to play baseball in Rockford. Spalding biographer Peter Levine notes that Spalding considered baseball "the only bright skies for me in those dark days of utter loneliness" as a child in Rockford.[2] By age 15, he was playing for the local Pioneers team. His fame burst out in Chicago and nationally when his pitching for the Forest Citys led to the only defeat of the National club of Washington during their groundbreaking 1867 Western Tour.

Ross Barnes, one of the great overlooked legends of nineteenth-century baseball, was a boyhood neighbor and close friend of Albert's. He was his baseball teammate in Rockford, Boston, and Chicago. While in Boston he joined with Louis Mahn to manufacture baseballs, which soon became part of the early Spalding sports empire.

His mother, **Harriett Spalding**, provided all the $800 capital to establish his brother J. Walter Spalding and Albert's first sporting goods store at 118 Randolph Street in Chicago in 1876.

His brother-in-law **William Thayer Brown** of Rockford, son of a local banker, provided the capital that enabled the Spaldings to purchase their first bat factory in Hastings, Michigan. He was married to Albert's sister **Mary**.[3]

Elizabeth "Lizzie" Churchill (Mayer) Spalding of Rockford was Albert's first true love. They were engaged in Rockford, broke it off, each married another, had an affair that included a child, and, after the death of both of their spouses, were married in 1900. Lizzie is why Albert moved to San Diego. After breaking up with Spalding in Rockford, Elizabeth married George Mayer and settled in Fort Wayne, Indiana. She taught at the Fort Wayne Conservatory of Music. She had moved to San Diego to become director of the Isis Conservatory of Music at Lomaland in 1897.[4]

William D. Page was Elizabeth's uncle. He became Spalding's business representative. In 1909, he and his family moved to Point Loma from Fort Wayne, where William had been the founder of the *Fort Wayne News*, the postmaster in Fort Wayne, and a leader in the local Republican Party. He managed Spalding's California Senate campaign. He and his brother Charles were part of the group that formed the San Diego Securities Company in 1911, which developed the Loma Portal community.

Charles T. Page was William's brother and another uncle of Lizzie's from Rockford.

Page played on the Forest City team prior to its professionalization with Spalding and Barnes. Spalding,

Barnes, and Page ate together, played together and sometimes slept in the same bed during those Rockford baseball days. Spalding often stayed at the Page home, and William and Charles referred to Spalding's mother as "Mother Spalding."[5] Page became a successful businessman in Rockford, Chicago, and Atlanta. While in Chicago, Page purchased a block of the Cubs stock, supported by Spalding.[6]

BOSTON AND CHICAGO

Spalding spent five years in Boston from 1871 through 1875. He and fellow Rockford native Barnes joined Harry and George Wright to make the Boston Red Stockings the dominant baseball team in America during the life of the National Association. Boston provided Spalding with the connections he needed to dominate early baseball equipment sales. He purchased the sporting goods operations of Wright & Ditson, Peck & Snyder in New York, and Al Reach in Philadelphia, as well as the patent for the Mahn baseball in Boston.

Two other important parts of Spalding's life also had origins in Boston. Spalding married Sarah Josephine Keith, who was from a respected Boston-area family. And in the winter of 1874, Harry Wright sent Spalding to England to arrange a baseball tour there. Wright, a former star cricket player, wanted to show the Brits how to play American baseball. The Red Stockings and the Athletics of Philadelphia traveled to Liverpool, where they played the first game between American professional baseball teams outside of the United States.[7] The impression of this first world tour and its purpose helped change Spalding's worldview from provincial to international.

When the National League organized in 1876, William Hulbert lured Spalding back to Chicago with the promise of $2,000 and 25 percent of the Chicago White Stockings' gate receipts. Spalding had also received, in 1876 with the help of Hulbert, the contract to exclusively produce the "official League book." He also produced a supplemental publication, *Spalding's Official Baseball Guide*.[8] In 1887 *The Sporting News* claimed that his Michigan plants were producing a million baseball bats a year. Separate factories also produced equipment for other sports.[9] In Chicago, Albert Spalding became a very wealthy man, baseball's first millionaire. San Diego benefited from this great wealth.

Spalding left Chicago for Theosophical reasons. His marriage in 1900 to the widowed Elizabeth Churchill Mayer, his long-time love, at Point Loma, California, signaled that he was heading west. Lizzie Spalding was

Albert Spalding, baseball magnate.

an important participant in the American Theosophical movement.

THEOSOPHY

The word theosophy derives from *theos* and *sophia*, the Greek words for God and wisdom. Its speculative thoughts can derive from mystical insights or from an analysis of comparative religions. Many variations of such groups arose throughout the world that were frowned upon by the Catholic and Protestant churches.[10]

The Theosophical Society was created by Madame Blavatsky, a Russian who wanted "to make an experimental comparison between spiritualism and the magic of the ancients." The original objectives, somewhat watered down later, were "to oppose the materialism of science and every form of dogmatic theology, especially the Christian." The final goal was to promote "a Brotherhood of Humanity."[11]

In 1884, Madame Blavatsky's reputation was damaged by charges that she had instructed some employees in the use of trickery to simulate psychic phenomena. It led to splits and struggles for control of the movement, both in the United States and internationally.[12] Capitalizing upon the dissent, and ultimately gaining control of the American part of the movement, was Katherine Tingley.[13] Once her authority was established in 1896, she proclaimed her vision of a "white city" that "would serve as the headquarters of the Theosophical Society and a place where the theosophical way of life could be realized," in the words of Emmett Greenwalt, author of *California Utopia: Point Loma: 1897–1942*.[14]

Needing a dramatic story to flip the Society from its New York City roots to a small city in southern California, she told of a meeting in New York with the famed explorer and politician John C. Fremont, who died in 1890. Tingley describes the revelation that came from Fremont:

I told him this story, this fairy story, that in the golden land, far away, by the blue Pacific, I thought as a child that I could fashion a city and bring the people of all countries together and have the youth taught how to live, and how to become true and strong and noble, and forceful royal warriors for humanity. "But," I said, "all that has passed; it is a closed book, and I question if it will ever be realized." He said: "There are some parts of your story that attract me very much. It is your description of this place where you are going to build your city. Have you ever been to California?" "No," I answered. "Well," he said, "the city you have described is a place that I know exists." And he then told of Point Loma. He was the first to name the place to me.[15]

SPALDING ARRIVES AT LOMALAND: 1900

Juan Rodriguez Cabrillo, a conquistador, was the first European explorer to land on the West Coast of the United States in 1542. The National Park Service believes that Cabrillo landed on the east shore of Point Loma, near the current Cabrillo National Monument. After the initial Spanish landing, it was 227 years before the Spanish created a settlement in California. They had been preoccupied with establishing control in areas to the south. The missionary responsibility was eventually tasked to the Franciscans, with Father Junipero Serra in charge. After landing with the ship *San Antonio* in San Diego Bay, Serra established the first of the nine missions that he personally founded.[16] San Diego de Alcala was dedicated on July 16, 1769. San Diego's Pacific Coast League and major-league baseball teams were named for the Franciscan fathers.

When Albert Spalding first arrived in San Diego in 1900 it was a historic but sleepy small city. Rockford had a larger population than San Diego until 1910. The military was just beginning to establish a foothold in San Diego as it began to look increasingly toward the Pacific. The two major tourist attractions in 1900, in addition to the temperate climate and the beaches, were the Hotel del Coronado, which had opened in 1888, and Lomaland, the developing Theosophist compound on Point Loma, which was dedicated in 1897.[17]

Albert and his first wife, Josie, had their primary residence in Chicago but she summered along Rumson Road at Sea Bright, New Jersey, from 1890 until she died there in July 1899.[18] The summer mansions of many of America's wealthiest families made Rumson Road and the Jersey Shore among the nation's most prestigious addresses during that period.[19]

In June 1900, Albert married Lizzie Mayer, his former fiancée, at his wife's residence at Lomaland.[20] Spalding clearly did not marry Mayer and move to Lomaland to receive lots of positive press clippings. A feature story in the *San Francisco Examiner* is an example of mocking coverage that followed him after he joined the colony. A large drawing of Spalding sitting on a horse with a sketch of his new home at Lomaland covering its body is headlined "Leaves Baseball for Mysticism" and captioned "Forsakes Baseball for Theosophy." One of the articles underneath is titled "Spalding Becomes Theosophist by Marriage: Famous Athlete, Converted by His Wife, Has Become a Member of the Tingley School of Mystery at Point Loma."[21]

The most famous controversy regarding Lomaland was the establishment of a Raja yoga school there. Another involved allegations of child abuse. Immediately after the Spanish-American War, Katherine Tingley began sending the first Cuban children to Point Loma. In his book *Baseball in the Garden of Eden*, John Thorn points out that since many adults joining Lomaland were childless or elderly, Cuba "could provide a stock of orphans, as well as children whose

Souvenir booklet distributed by Lomaland at the Panama-California Exposition.

parents wished them to be educated in America. …It would not be long before the majority of students at Point Loma were Cuban."[22]

In 1902, a group of Cuban children was detained at Ellis Island at the request of the New York Society for the Prevention of Cruelty to Children. The immigration hearing tarred the Point Loma institution and a furious Spalding was questioned about charges such as children being given only limited food and mothers being prevented from seeing their children. The New York hearing went against Lomaland. Had the ruling stood, Cuban children would have been prevented from going to the compound to be educated, and Lomaland's reputation would have been ruined. But the decision was overturned in Washington. The state of California investigated the school and gave it positive reviews.[23]

Spalding, when asked his views on Theosophy, generally described it in terms of his wife's passion and that he "married into it." He told the *San Francisco Examiner*, "I find here at Point Loma many educated, cultured, refined and most genial people, certainly the equal of, and perhaps superior to, any I ever met anywhere." He continued, "I am not, however, so ardent a Theosophist as Mrs. Spalding." But he gave a qualified endorsement of its worldly work: "If all these things and more which I might mention, make me a theosophist, I am perfectly willing to stand for it."[24]

While living on Point Loma, Spalding's last big baseball project was the creation of a prestigious commission to rebut the argument that baseball was not a truly American original game. In 1907, it ordained Major Abner Doubleday as the inventor of baseball in Cooperstown, New York. As all baseball historians know, that is false. There is no established record that Doubleday was even interested in baseball. He was, however, a Theosophist.

In 1873, Doubleday retired from his military career and settled in New Jersey. There he became active in the Theosophical Society, becoming president of the American operations in 1878. Doubleday's active participation in the Society could have smoothed his way to becoming the rather mystical founder of baseball in the eyes of the Spalding Commission.

ALBERT SPALDING: SAN DIEGO BOOMER

Spalding played a key role in shaping San Diego. A postcard from 1914 shows the city from a perspective just east of the developing Balboa Park, looking toward the ocean. In the distance, the entrance to San Diego Bay has mostly barren Point Loma forming the north side and on the south side is the Silver Strand,

1914 postcard with Point Loma on upper right.

a narrow sand isthmus, and Coronado Island. On the high ground, barely visible out on the peninsula, is Lomaland, standing mostly alone, eight miles from San Diego.

Lomaland was not a pejorative term given to the Theosophy campus but how it referred to itself. As noted, it was a significant tourism draw. Daily excursions to the site came from Hotel del Coronado and other hotels in the region. A souvenir booklet was created for visitors: *Lomaland Souvenir: Panoramic View of the International Theosophical Headquarters Grounds with a glimpse of Greek Theater*. The booklet's photos include the "Raja-Yoga College and Aryan Memorial Temple from the West," as well as photos of the first Greek amphitheater built in the United States Nor did Lomaland hide its students, featuring photos of the children and an explanation of its educational mission. On page nine, the booklet mentions: "To the north is one of the residences, the first one erected in Lomaland, leased by Mr. A.G. Spalding."[25]

Included on the 132 acres of Lomaland was Spalding's first project, his new home. Marc Lamster, an architecture critic who wrote a book on Spalding's world tour, described it as "an oriental fantasy, an octagonal structure with an external spiral staircase, extensive internal carvings, and a crystal on the roof."[26] The Spalding home survives as the administrative building of Point Loma Nazarene University.

In 1903, just north of his two-story, gleaming white showplace, Spalding developed a "fanciful, cliff-side Japanese garden."[27] He spent an estimated $2 million

($55 million in today's dollars) constructing his park.[28] Most of its structures slid into the Pacific Ocean from erosion or were undermined by dangerous ocean-carved caves. The remaining structures were removed because they had accelerated cliff erosion that was naturally occurring. Spalding's efforts did result in the area being preserved as one of the few stretches of undeveloped coast in San Diego, Sunset Cliffs Natural Park.[29]

In 1912, Spalding built his Point Loma Club nine-hole golf course. It was one of the first golf courses in San Diego, preceded only by those at Hotel del Coronado and within Balboa Park.[30] Its dramatic elevation changes provide golfers with panoramic views of the downtown skyline and the harbor.[31] Spalding built his course where Point Loma began to rise, about three miles southeast of his home. The Point Loma Golf Club merged with the San Diego Country Club in 1914. The San Diego Country Club again separated in 1921, moving to Chula Vista.[32]

HOW THE PANAMA CANAL TRANSFORMED SAN DIEGO

The Spanish-American War led to Cuba becoming a protectorate of the United States. The Philippines were

2. The Bridge, Sunset Cliffs, San Diego, Cal.

Sunset Cliffs on Point Loma, developed by Spalding, was a major visitor attraction.

Club House of Spalding's Point Loma Golf Club.

also purchased from Spain. Not only did this lead to Cuban children coming to Lomaland as students, but also to the United States taking over the development of the Panama Canal in order to protect its territorial interests, promote trade, and utilize its increased naval power.

"Apart from wars, it represented the largest, most costly single effort ever before mounted anywhere on earth," wrote historian David McCullough. "It was both the crowning constructive effort of the Victorian Era and the first grandiose and assertive show of American power at the dawn of the new century. And yet the passage of the first ship through the canal in the summer of 1914—the first voyage through the American landmass—marked the resolution of a dream as old as the voyages of Columbus."[33]

During the late nineteenth century, world's fairs began to gather American attention beyond New York, especially after the success of the *World's Columbian Exhibition of 1893* in Chicago. Business leaders of the San Diego Chamber of Commerce sought to seize the opportunity that geography presented: San Diego Bay was the first port that ships would encounter in the United States when steaming north after traversing the Panama Canal.

In 1909, the Panama-California Exposition Company was formed to seek official designation and funding. San Diego was the smallest city ever to attempt an exposition. U.S. Grant Jr. was named president. Spalding served as a vice president along with John D. Spreckels, L.S. McClure, and G. Aubrey Davidson, the president of the San Diego Chamber of Commerce who had developed the proposal to hold an exposition.[34]

The effort to attract, plan, and execute the Panama-Pacific Exposition led to immediate population growth in San Diego County, from 37,000 to over 100,000 by the time the exposition opened in 1915. The wealthy business patrons had already begun building roads and rail tracks but they lacked a focal point for their efforts. The exposition gave them one. First, however, they had to fight off San Francisco's attempt to seize the exhibition. Lyman Gage had led the rescue effort in Chicago when New York attempted to subvert Chicago's effort to land the 1893 World's Fair. After serving as Secretary of the Treasury from 1897 to 1902, Gage, a convert to Theosophy, built a house in La Playa, approximately 2,000 feet from his friend Spalding. He then assisted San Diego in maintaining its host designation, shared with San Francisco.

Spalding, Spreckels, and E. W. Scripps were named San Diego County road commissioners by the Board of Supervisors in 1909. Spreckels was the wealthiest man in San Diego. Anchoring his wealth was a steamship company critical to developing trade with the South Pacific, specifically sugar from Hawaii. Among other things, he owned the Hotel del Coronado and the *San Diego Union*. Scripps, head of the Scripps-Howard newspaper chain, owned substantial land east of La Jolla.

The three men, referred to as the "Triple S" commission, led a coordinated city effort to transform itself beyond just roads. In 1907 Spalding, Spreckels, and Scripps had responded to a request from two other San Diego leaders who came to them for significant financial assistance to purchase the 14 lots comprising Presidio Hill, the historic grounds of Father Serra's first mission. Perhaps the baseball team would not be called the Padres had this site been lost to development.[35]

The Exposition coalition battled between those who wanted it to be held on the waterfront and those who wanted to develop the central city park space. The park was selected and renamed Balboa Park. The predominant style of its major structures led to the creation of

Promotional brochure for the 1915 Panama-California Exhibition.

an adapted Spanish Colonial, Mediterranean style that has become identified with San Diego and much of California. An example outside Balboa Park is the Santa Fe Railroad Depot in downtown San Diego, which opened in 1915 to accommodate Expo visitors. This style was a major change from the neo-classical domination of previous Fairs, including the Palace of Fine Arts in the San Francisco Panama-Pacific Exposition.

A 2,300-foot pleasure street called the Isthmus was the primary attraction for visitors at Balboa Park. Sights along the way included a 6,000-foot rollercoaster and a 250-foot replica of the Panama Canal, with ships moving up and down through locks.[36] The Isthmus Zoo was such a popular attraction that during the Expo, a Zoological Society was organized. They purchased the Isthmus animals and, in 1916, opened the world-famous San Diego Zoo in Balboa Park.[37]

SPALDING FOR US SENATE

In 1910, the business leaders of San Diego pushed Spalding to run for the United States Senate. In many ways, Spalding was a progressive, but he was opposed by the Lincoln-Roosevelt Club, which controlled the Progressive movement. The progressives chose John D. Works as their candidate for Senate partly because of his popularity in the temperance movement and his leadership of the Good Government League of Los Angeles.[38] The dominant force in California politics at the time was the Southern Pacific Railroad's Political Bureau, which the progressives were determined to defeat.[39]

Spalding narrowly lost the non-binding primary 64,757 to 63,182.[40] The Progressive forces won the majority of the Republican nominations, including the overwhelming majority of the 428 delegates for the Republican state convention.[41] However, in 1910 it was still the state legislators who selected senators. They chose Works over Spalding 92–21. Spalding supporters were irate since he had carried the majority of the counties, which theoretically would have given him a decisive 75 pledged legislators. But the primary vote was advisory, not binding.[42] The progressives had swept the field, as illustrated by the convention domination. They clearly opposed Spalding.

Spalding campaign manager William Page, his wife's uncle, was outraged. *The 1911 Spalding Guide* includes a three-page tirade about the "rape of a people's direct primary law." Page accurately points out that Works underperformed Progressive ballot leader Hiram Johnson. He also notes the double-standard of the Progressive forces' denunciations of bossism and then offering "deals" to override the presumed preferences of primary voters. Page further proves the hostility of the Progressive leaders to Spalding by listing the extreme tactics they used to block Spalding's nomination. It might have been a "monstrous wickedness," or at least inside hardball, but it was legal.[43]

Spalding dropped out of key area positions after his loss, including the Roads Commission and the Panama-Pacific Exposition board, but he remained active. He continued developing Sunset Cliffs Park. He started his golf course near the entrance to the Loma Portal community in 1912. They both were attractions during the Exposition. He became president of San Diego Securities in 1912, a position he held until his unexpected death in 1915. It developed the Loma Portal neighborhood, which opened in 1913 in time to capitalize on the Panama Expo. The board of directors included the Page uncles as well as George Burnham, who became a vice president of the Expo after Spalding withdrew. Colonel Charlie Collier financed the trolley that came to the entrance of the area, which enabled it to attract home buyers as well as visitors for Spalding's other Point Loma ventures.[44] Collier was selected by the original Panama-Pacific board, including Spalding, to be director-general of the Expo in 1909. He chose Balboa Park as the site and oversaw the project.

In other words, while Spalding lost the Senate race, he remained active until the end of his life in helping reshape the face of San Diego.[45] ■

Notes

1. Bill McMahon, "Al Spalding," SABR BioProject, https://sabr.org/bioproj/person/b99355e0.
2. Peter Levine, *A.G. Spalding and the Rise of Baseball: The Promise of American Sport* (New York and Oxford: Oxford University Press, 1985), 5.
3. Levine, *A.G. Spalding and the Rise of Baseball*, 82–3.
4. John Thorn, *Baseball in the Garden of Eden: The Secret History of the Early Sport* (New York: Simon & Schuster, 2011), 207–26.
5. Ronald V. May, RPA; "Historical Nomination of the Minnie Scheibe/Bathrick Brothers Speculation House, Loma Portal," Historic House Research for the California Department of Parks and Recreation, November 2016, 18–20.
6. "Buffrey Tells of Charles T. Page, Prominent Atlanta Man Is Dean of All Southern Baseball Exponents and Was One of the First to Bring National Game to South," Atlanta Constitution, August 10, 1919.
7. Christopher Devine, Harry Wright, *The Father of Professional Baseball* (Jefferson, NC: McFarland, 2003), 104–5; see also Mark Souder, "When Boston Dominated Baseball" in Baseball's First Nine, ed. Bob LeMoine and Bill Nowlin (Phoenix: SABR, 2016), 18–20.
8. Levine, *A.G. Spalding and the Rise of Baseball*, 75.
9. Levine, 79.
10. Emmett A. Greenwalt, *California Utopia: Point Loma: 1897–1942* (San Diego: Point Loma Publications, 1978), 1.
11. Greenwalt, 3.
12. Greenwalt, 5–11.
13. Greenwalt, 12–22.
14. Greenwalt, 19.
15. Greenwalt, 19.
16. Kevin Starr, *California: A History* (New York: Modern Library, 2005), 31–39
17. La Playa Trail Association, *Images of America: Point Loma* (Charleston, S.C.: Arcadia Publishing, 2016), 48.
18. "Mrs. Spalding's Death at Seabright," *New York Tribune*, July 11, 1890.
19. Greg Kelly, "Monmouth Beach: Land of Rich& Famous," *Monmouth Beach Life*, March 16, 2019. http://www.monmouthbeachlife.com/mb-history/monmouth-beach-once-land-of-rich-famous/.
20. "Mayer-Spalding," *Los Angeles Times*, June 24, 1900.
21. "Leaves Baseball for Mysticism," *San Francisco Examiner*, March 29, 1903.
22. Thorn, *Baseball in the Garden of Eden*, 265.
23. Thorn, 270–71.
24. "Leaves Baseball for Mysticism."
25. Katherine Tingley, *Lomaland Souvenir: Panoramic View of the International Theosophical Headquarters Grounds with a glimpse of Greek Theater* (San Diego: Theosophical Society), 1912.
26. Marc Lamster, "The Curious Architecture of Albert Spalding," Design Observer, August 10, 2009. https://designobserver.com/feature/the-curious-architecture-of-albert-spalding/19878).
27. Cecilia Rasmussen, "San Diego Theosophists Had Own Ideas on a New Age," *Los Angeles Times*, August 3, 2003.
28. This dollar figure likely includes his golf course because I could not locate a separate number.
29. "Sunset Cliffs History," Sunset Cliffs Natural Park. http://www.famosaslough.org/schis.htm; "Sunset Cliffs Natural Park," City of San Diego Park and Recreation Department. http://www.famosaslough.org/scgraphics/SCNPbrochure.pdf
30. "SCGA History," Southern California Golf Association. http://www.scga.org/about/scgahistory/part-1.
31. "Sail Ho Golf Club," San Diego Golf Pages. http://www.golfsd.com/sail_ho.html.
32. http://www.thelomaclub.com/.
33. David McCullough, *The Path Between the Seas: The Creation of the Panama Canal, 1870–1914* (New York: Simon & Schuster, 1977), 11–12.
34. Richard W. Amero, *Balboa Park and the 1915 Exposition* (Charleston, S.C.: History Press, 2013), 14.
35. "Presidio Park: A Statement of George W. Marston in 1942," *Journal of San Diego History* 32, no. 2 (Spring 1986). http://www.sandiegohistory.org/journal/1986/april/presidio/.
36. Amero, *Balboa Park and the 1915 Exposition*, 59–60.
37. Amero, 139.
38. Spencer C. Olin Jr., "Hiram Johnson, the Lincoln-Roosevelt League, and the Election of 1910," *California Historical Society Quarterly* 45, no. 3 (September 1966): 225–40.
39. Martin Shefter, "Regional Receptivity to Reform: The Legacy of the Progressive Era," *Political Science Quarterly* 98, no. 3 (Autumn 1983): 471.
40. Levine, *A.G. Spalding and the Rise of Baseball*, 141.
41. Olin, "Hiram Johnson," 235.
42. "Primaries Favor Spalding, Captures Majority of Counties in California Senate Race," *New York Tribune*, September 6, 1910.
43. William D. Page, "A Political Crime," *Spalding's Official Base Ball Guide*, March 1911.
44. May, "Historical Nomination of the Minnie Scheibe/Bathrick Brothers Speculation House," 11–21.
45. Amero, *Balboa Park and the 1915 Exposition*, 14–15

The Shared National Pastime

San Diego's First Japanese Ball Game

Robert K. Fitts

Since the mid-nineteenth century, baseball has helped immigrants assimilate into American society. By following their local team or taking the diamond, foreigners improve their English, become part of the cultural fabric, and learn American values. Between the mid-1890s and 1910, over 100,000 Japanese people settled in the United States. Like other immigrant groups, they struggled with bigotry and language barriers as they adapted to their new environment. But unlike other immigrants, many Japanese were already familiar with baseball. The sport would serve as a bridge between the two cultures, bringing people together with the shared love of the game.

American teachers introduced the game to Japan in the early 1870s. The sport was limited to elite schools and clubs in Tokyo and Kobe until schoolboys from Daiichi Koto Gakko (the First Higher School), commonly known by its nickname, Ichiko, upset an American adult team from the Yokohama Country Club in a series of games in 1896. After the Japanese victory, teams sprang up on high school and college campuses across the country.

Having learned the game in Japan, many Issei (Japanese immigrants) longed to continue playing. Excluded from most white American teams, they formed their own clubs. Between 1903 and 1905, Issei established the Fuji Athletic and Kanagawa Doshi Clubs in San Francisco, the Japanese Base Ball Club of Los Angeles, and Nippon Baseball Club in Seattle.[1]

In the spring of 1905, the Waseda University baseball club from Tokyo became the first foreign team to tour the United States. It played 26 games mostly against college and semi-pro teams in California, Oregon, and Washington. Fans packed ballparks to watch the novel team and newspapers covered the games with extensive articles. Waseda's popularity introduced Japanese baseball to white Americans and turned many Issei into baseball fans and players.[2]

Inspired by the publicity surrounding the Waseda University tour, Guy Green, the owner of the barnstorming Nebraska Indians team, decided to create a barnstorming team of Japanese players. He recruited a squad of Issei from the West Coast and sent them on a 150-plus-game tour of the Midwest during the summer of 1906. They would be the first professional Japanese team on either side of the Pacific.[3]

Returning to Los Angeles, members of Green's squad decided to form their own team known as the Nanka (meaning Southern California) Baseball Club under the leadership of Atsuyoshi "Harry" Saisho. The son of a samurai who had fought against Takamori Saigo during the 1877 Satsuma Rebellion (the war was the basis for the romanticized Tom Cruise movie *The Last Samurai*), Saisho had learned the American game while at school in Miyazaki on Japan's southern island of Kyushu. In 1903, Saisho emigrated to California with dreams of attending Stanford University. Finding his English inadequate to enroll, he drifted between menial jobs before settling in Los Angeles.

The Nanka played against amateur and semipro white and black teams nearly every weekend and attracted the area's top Japanese players. "We were crazy about baseball," recalled infielder Kiichi Suzuki. "Nothing was more interesting than playing baseball on Sundays and holidays when we were young. We never took jobs that would prevent us from taking Sunday off, no matter how good the opportunity was."[4]

In early 1909, Saisho's team decided to turn professional and barnstorm across the States as the Japanese Base Ball Association (J.B.B.A.). They began in California but after embarrassing losses to an amateur team in Riverside, the African American LA Giants, and Los Angeles High School, they dissolved the squad. Suzuki noted that the team was "enthusiastic but incompetent."[5]

Six months later, when the African American Occidentals from Salt Lake City visited Los Angeles, Jesse Orndorff, the catcher for the Pacific Coast League's Los Angeles Angels, organized a game between the Occidentals and the city's top Japanese players. The *Los Angeles Herald* ran articles on the event for two straight weeks, noting that "the baseball game…is an exhibition of the national game in which race

ATHLETIC PARK 26ᵀᴴ & NAT **Baseball**
SUNDAY, FEBRUARY 27, at 2:30 P. M.
JAPANESE ORIENTALS vs. SAN DIEGO
Take Logan Avenue Car to 26th and Main Streets
Admission 25c · · Grand Stand 25c

Advertisement for the San Diego game from the *San Diego Union*, February 27, 1910.

supremacy in the art will be settled."[6] Two thousand fans came out to watch. Although Saisho and some of his best players dropped out of the game at the last minute, the excitement surrounding the event prompted Saisho to reunite the J.B.B.A. and continue the club's quest to turn professional.

In late December 1909, Saisho traveled to San Diego to arrange games for the squad. The *San Diego Union* reported, "Saisho says he realizes that the San Diego Midwinter league team would be too fast a proposition for his countrymen but that he would like to play any amateur or semi-professional aggregation of hit and run artists."[7]

The games, however, did not materialize and Saisho later tried to schedule a game for February. This time, he intended to combine the baseball game with a wrestling match. The *Union* wrote:

Harry A. Saisho, the polite little Japanese who was in San Diego about two months ago is now developing into a manager of wrestlers. …Saisho's English is a trifle faulty, but his intentions are good. His letter…is reproduced below in full:

Sporting Editor, San Diego Union:

Dear Sir:

I am much obliged to you helped us as much as possible past time. I trying to get game (baseball) now in Feb. or first March if possible for we may not stay any longer than March. Here is another sporting matter. My friend Mr. R. [Ryo] Fukada, that jujitsu wrestler—he matched to Young Johnson, middleweight champion of coast and won about 9 minutes, Jan. 4th at Los Angeles. He willing to get one fight to a wrestler in San Diego in recent. He will be here in a few days. Please let me know a man attend on. He weight about 140 pounds or more. I believe he is more stronger than Yokohama called a world champion. Please notify soon possible.

– Harry A. Saisho[8]

The letter worked and Saisho arranged both a ballgame and a match for Fukuda, a Japanese-born Harvard student, for late February.[9]

A week before the game, San Diego's newspapers began running advertisements and articles on the upcoming event. A large crowd was expected as it would be "the first time the fans have ever had the chance of seeing a Japanese team of baseball players in action." The *Union* reported, "The Japs are now playing a fast game of ball and should be able to give the locals a run for their money. The little brown men are said to be exceptionally fast at fielding and running bases and in previous games have demonstrated their ability to keep the man behind the bat constantly on the alert."[10]

The J.B.B.A. featured some of the top Issei ballplayers in the country. Saisho's childhood friend Ken Kitsuse played shortstop. Just under 5-foot-3 and 115 pounds with a boyish face, he was often mistaken for a child by opposing players and fans. But he could "field like a cat" and run the bases like a demon.[11] Kitsuse was a natural athlete, excelling at judo, kendo, and long-distance running as well as being the best Japanese ballplayer on the West Coast. Teammate Kiichi Suzuki remembered, "We considered him the god of baseball. When somebody made a mistake, he

Atsuyoshi "Harry" Saisho

would give him hell [or in Japanese, 'drop thunder']. For this reason, we called him Thunder."[12]

The fleet Minoru Sohara, another of Saisho's childhood friends, played left field. Although not much of a hitter, he could field his position well and was an expert with the sword, often entertaining fans with pregame demonstrations with his gleaming katana or wooden bokuto. Suzuki played second base. From Chiba, just east of Tokyo, Suzuki had played on the Waseda University practice team (similar to a junior varsity), learning the game from Japan's best players. Filling out the squad was Toyo Fujita at first, a former member of Guy Green's Japanese barnstorming team; Riichiro Shiraishi in right field; and Morii in center. Saisho would play third base.

The J.B.B.A. would have its hands full. The San Diego squad had won the California Winter League championship for the past two seasons and would win the next two as well. The team featured at least two big-leaguers—third baseman Tom Downey, who played for Cincinnati from 1909 to 1911, and first baseman Chick Autry, his Reds teammate. To be competitive, Saisho recruited two ringers. Orndorff of the Angels would catch while Jim Scott of the Chicago White Sox would take the mound. The 21-year-old had just finished his rookie season, going 12–12 with a 2.30 ERA. He would pitch for nine years in Chicago, winning 107 games, and accompany the White Sox on their 1913 visit to Japan.

Despite threatening rain, fans crowded into Athletic Park on Sunday, February 20, filling the covered wooden grandstand behind home plate and the bleachers down

the foul lines. All were eager for the novel game. Yet game time came and went without the Japanese taking the field. Seeing the weather report in a Los Angeles newspaper, Saisho had assumed the game would be canceled and kept his team at home. A flurry of telegrams identified the misunderstanding and rescheduled the game for the following week.[13]

Anticipation grew during the ensuing week. The Japanese "will interest many of the fans who have read of the exploits of the mikado's subjects in the national game," noted the *San Diego Union*.[14] Fans were particularly excited to see Scott pitch. To prevent another misunderstanding, San Diego manager Will H. Palmer telephoned Saisho on Thursday night confirming the game.

On Saturday, February 26, Saisho and most of the team arrived in San Diego for Fukuda's wrestling match, to be held that evening at Arizona Hall. Prior to the main event, the ballclub's left fielder, Minoru Soharu, challenged local fencing expert K. Suzuki in a kendo match—the first held in the city. Afterward, Fukuda faced amateur wrestling champion Tom Travers in the ring. The rules were simple. Travers could use any style of grappling he wished, but Fukuda was limited to jiujitsu holds and throws. The first to fall twice would lose. Strangely, despite extensive pre-match newspaper coverage, the result of the bout is not recorded in local papers.[15]

The following afternoon, fans once again packed Athletic Park to watch the Japanese play the local champions. Once again, the fans had to wait. The Santa Fe train from Los Angeles, carrying Scott, Orndorff and

The Japanese Base Ball Association in 1911.

two Japanese players, was delayed. On the diamond, the players practiced as they waited. After an hour, Palmer and Saisho decided to entertain the fans with "a scrub game" until the missing players arrived. Palmer recruited local amateur players to fill out the Japanese team while San Diego's John Lambert took the mound for the Japanese against his usual teammates.

The contest, however, was completely one-sided. According to the *Union*, Saisho's team "at no time had a chance to win. At times the Japanese players showed their ability as fielders, but their batting was so weak that although [the San Diego pitcher] merely 'lobbed' the ball across the pan they were able to get but a few scratch hits." To entertain the crowd, the San Diego team "made the game one long joke [which] provided plenty of fun for the people in the grand stand and the bleachers." By the time the missing players arrived, "most of the spectators had left the grounds."

At 4PM, Scott took the mound for the J.B.B.A. and the feature game began in front of near-empty stands. The *Evening Tribune* noted, "The spectators who remained were well repaid for their long wait" as Scott dominated. Using a blazing fastball and sweeping curve, he struck out eight in just four innings before the game was called on account of darkness after only an hour of play. The "exhibition would probably have been one of the best of the season, had it started on time," lamented the newspaper.[16]

Although the game was a near disaster, it did not deter Saisho and his J.B.B.A. teammates from pursuing their dream to turn pro. The squad returned to Los Angeles, recruited several new players, and practiced.

The next spring, they embarked on a 150-game barnstorming tour of the Midwest, becoming the country's only professional Issei team. Later, the ballplayers would form their own teams, coaching the next generation as baseball became an integral part of Japanese American culture. ∎

Notes

1. Kerry Yo Nakagawa, *Japanese American Baseball in California* (Charleston, SC: History Press, 2014); Samuel O. Regalado, *Nikkei Baseball* (Urbana IL: University of Illinois Press, 2013).
2. Robert K. Fitts, "Baseball and the Yellow Peril: Waseda University's 1905 American Tour," in *Base Ball 10*, ed. Don Jensen (Jefferson, NC: McFarland, 2018), 141–59.
3. Fitts, "The First Japanese Professionals: Guy Green's 1906 Japanese Base Ball Team," *Nine* (forthcoming).
4. Masaru Akahori, *Nanka Nihonjin Yakyushi* [History of Japanese Baseball in Southern California] (Los Angeles: Town Crier, 1956), 4.
5. Akahori, *Nanka Nihonjin Yakyushi*, 3.
6. "Japanese vs. Negroes," *Los Angeles Herald*, December 18, 1909.
7. "Japanese Baseball Team Wants Games Here Christmas Day," *San Diego Union*, November 4, 1909.
8. "Jap Mat Artist Looks for Match," *San Diego Union*, January 14, 1910.
9. "San Diego Wrestler Will Meet Japanese," *San Diego Union*, February 19, 1910.
10. "Jap Base Ball team to Play Big Leaguers," *San Diego Evening Tribune*, February 19, 1910; "Little Brown Men to Play Local Team Today," *San Diego Union*, February 20, 1910.
11. "War with the Japanese is Over," *Audubon Country Journal*, August 31, 1911.
12. Akahori, *Nanka Nihonjin Yakyushi*, 12.
13. "Jap Aggregation Fails to Appear," *San Diego Union*, February 21, 1910.
14. "Will Try for Mat Honors Saturday," *San Diego Union*, February 25, 1910.
15. "San Diego Wrestler Will Meet Japanese," *San Diego Union*, February 19, 1910, 7.
16. "Scott Makes Hit with Fans by Speedy Work in Box," *San Diego Union*, February 28, 1910; "Scott Pitches Elegant Ball in Fast Game," *San Diego Evening Tribune*, February 28, 1910.

Charlie Schmutz

The First San Diego-Born Major Leaguer

Bill Lamb

With its temperate Pacific Coast climate and rich baseball tradition, San Diego has long been a spawning ground for major-league talent, sending some 121 of her sons to the bigs. The second, and by far the greatest, of these San Diegans was Ted Williams, whose march to Cooperstown began with the 1939 Boston Red Sox. But 25 years before the Splendid Splinter made his Sox debut, the trail to the majors for the San Diego-born ballplayer was blazed by a player as obscure as Williams is famous: Charlie Schmutz, a Deadball Era right-handed pitcher.

Schmutz's tenure with the 1914–15 National League Brooklyn Robins was brief (19 games), undistinguished (one victory), and quickly forgotten. In fact, during his lifetime, Schmutz was mostly known only to the baseball fans of Seattle, where he grew up and played the majority of his baseball. Nevertheless, Charlie Schmutz is the correct answer to the baseball trivia question: "Who was the first major-league player born in San Diego?"[1]

Charles Otto Schmutz was a New Year's Day baby, born on January 1, 1891. He was the oldest of three children born to streetcar conductor Frank J. Schmutz (1865–1948) and his teenage wife, Alice (nee Murphy, 1876–1958).[2] While Charlie was still in grade school, the family relocated to Seattle, the burgeoning seaport 1,250 miles to the north. As far as has been discovered, Schmutz never returned to the city of his birth. Rather, he became a lifelong Seattle resident. And it was there that Charlie Schmutz first attracted public notice.

Like other marginal major leaguers, Schmutz would be remembered not for his abbreviated time in big-league livery but for his schoolboy exploits. Indeed, the 1907 campaign of Schmutz and his teammates on the Seattle High School nine was celebrated locally for the succeeding 50 years. That Seattle High lineup was loaded with talent. Within a few years, star first baseman Charlie Mullen would begin a five-season major-league career. Three other team members, pitcher Jimmy "Toots" Agnew, third baseman Harry Martin, and memorably named left fielder Ten Million, went on to play minor-league ball, while catcher Mert

Hemenway, shortstop Ernie Maguire, and outfielders Bill "Wee" Coyle and Fred Hickenbottom would become varsity lettermen at the University of Washington.[3] In the beginning, 16-year-old freshman Charlie Schmutz auditioned for a spot in the overstocked SHS outfield, but he was slow-footed and a weak righty batsman.[4] He had imposing size, though—lanky but eventually near 6-foot-2, 195 pounds—and a strong throwing arm.[5] So he decided to give pitching a try. Although it would sometimes later be reported that Schmutz had a sizzling fastball, he initially threw "as slow as molasses in January." [6] But he made good use of a puzzling shot-put pitching motion and had somehow learned to throw a wicked spitball.

On April 17, 1907, Seattle High's novice pitcher made an astonishing debut. Matched in a preseason game against the professional Seattle Siwashes, a Class B Northwestern League club owned and managed by former major-league catcher Dan Dugdale, Schmutz shut them down on two hits, winning, 2–1. The local sports press was dumbfounded. "A long-legged lad named Schmutz, who had not been considered good enough for the high school team, pitched a great game and with the aid of a balk motion had the professionals buffaloed," reported the *Seattle Times*.[7] Meanwhile, the *Seattle Post-Intelligencer* informed readers that "Mr. Schmutz, a pitcher of the bean-pole variety…was the stumbling block that Seattle could not overcome. From the dizzy heights he handed them down so nicely shaded that only two hits were chalked against him."[8]

Overmatched area high school nines rarely provided much competition, but when the scholastic season was completed, Seattle High School embarked upon something far more ambitious: a transcontinental baseball tour. Such an excursion by a high school team was unprecedented, and the Seattle Board of Education was unenthused about sending teenage students on a two-month cross-country trip. But once a consortium of city businessmen agreed to finance the tour—seen as a useful vehicle for advertising the upcoming 1909 Alaska-Yukon-Pacific Exhibition—the board acquiesced, deputizing SHS faculty member

B.C. Hastings to chaperone the 11 players and student manager Harold Stewart on the trip.[9]

Arriving in Minnesota on June 17, the boys started off on the right foot, defeating the St. Paul Athletic Club, 2–1, behind a one-hit, 13-strikeout effort by Schmutz. Playing almost every day except Sundays, Seattle High played winning ball against the majority of its high school opponents in Chicago, Detroit, Baltimore, Washington, and Charlottesville, Virginia. After Schmutz no-hit D.C.'s Western High School, the unofficial schoolboy champs of the East, the local press questioned the age and amateur status of Seattle High team members.[10] Such skepticism prompted an indignant Hastings to declare that all the boys were high school students in good standing and that they had passed their June examinations before embarking on the trip.[11] Meanwhile, student manager Stewart produced the players' birth certificates, proving that none was over 18 years old.[12]

Seattle High fared less well against semipro and athletic club teams, dropping a 4–0 decision to the crack Frankfort (Philadelphia) AC and suffering a 5–4 loss to the Philadelphia Colored Giants on successive days in early July. But overall, the youngsters held their own against older, more seasoned opposition, even notching three consecutive wins over a fast semipro club in Abilene, Texas. By the time the 8,600-mile tour was completed, Seattle High had compiled a respectable 16–15 record against all comers, with almost all of these games having been pitched by Schmutz or

fellow freshman Jimmy Agnew.[13] Greeted at the train station by more than 1,000 locals upon their arrival home, the boys were the toast of Seattle and the recipients of an officially hosted parade through city streets.[14]

Schmutz, Mullen, Agnew, and most of the other tour players returned to the Seattle High lineup in 1908, achieving mixed results.[15] On April 7, the Seattle Siwashes got their revenge against the high schoolers, driving Schmutz from the mound in the third inning on their way to a 5–0 victory.[16] Playing a mostly high school schedule that also included games against the University of Idaho and Washington State varsities (both losses) and a 7–1 Schmutz triumph over the University of Washington, the SHS nine won more often than they lost, but were no longer the area's baseball wunderkinds. During the ensuing summer, Schmutz, Mullen, and company played for their own self-organized amateur team, the Nationals. Then, in the autumn, Schmutz and Agnew pitched semipro ball, mostly for a local team called the Websters.[17]

Resisting pressure to turn fully professional, Schmutz resumed double-duty high school and semipro ball pitching in the spring of 1909.[18] Websters club owner Joe Schlumpf was glad to have Schmutz back, but could not understand why Seattle Turks (nee Siwashes) owner-manager Dugdale had not made the effort necessary to sign the 18-year-old hurler. Said Schlumpf, "In my judgment, [Schmutz] is the best youngster that has ever played western baseball."[19] One thing, however, had changed. When Schmutz took

SEATTLE TIMES

The 1907 Seattle High School team. Charlie Schmutz stands in back row, farthest left. Seated directly in front of Schmutz is future major leaguer Charlie Mullen.

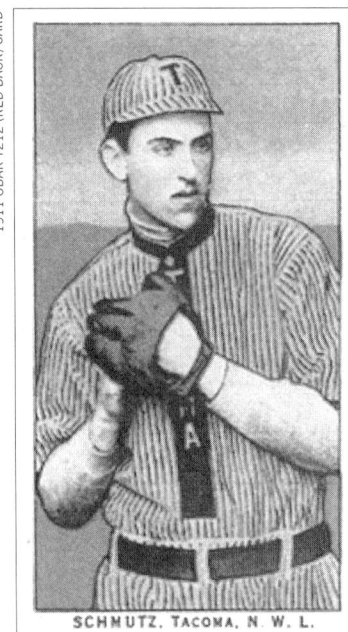

SCHMUTZ. TACOMA. N. W. L.

Schmutz obtained much needed seasoning pitching for Tacoma of the Northwestern League during the 1910–12 seasons.

the mound for a high school game, he now wore the uniform of Seattle's Abraham Lincoln High School.[20] The 1909 scholastic campaign ended with Schmutz pitching Lincoln to a 4–0 victory over Broadway (formerly Seattle) High and "old pal" Jimmy Agnew, thereby capturing the high school championship of the Northwest for his new school.[21]

Schmutz left Lincoln at the completion of his junior year and never earned a high school diploma.[22] Once it was clear that Schmutz's school days were behind him, rumors re-circulated that he would soon be joining the Northwestern League Tacoma Tigers. Such reports proved unfounded. Charlie remained home in Seattle long enough to perform an act of heroism. While canoeing on Lake Washington, he and a friend rescued a drowning young woman.[23] Schmutz spent the remainder of the summer pitching semipro ball in Dillon, Montana.[24] Upon returning home, he joined his teenage brother Ernie in the employ of a Seattle grocery store.[25]

In 1910, 19-year-old Charlie Schmutz finally entered the professional ranks, signing with Tacoma. His pro debut, however, was delayed by a case of blood poisoning that required several days' hospitalization.[26] But once he regained his health, Schmutz became a Tacoma staff mainstay. In 39 games, he posted a 14–20 (.412) record for the 73–84 (.465) Tigers, striking out 120 while walking 81 in 299⅓ innings.[27] He returned to Tacoma the following season, going 14–14 in 33 games for an 81–84 club, attracting major-league attention in the process.[28] That August, it was reported that Schmutz was one of three Northwestern League hurlers signed by retired star Bill Lange for the Cincin-

nati Reds.[29] Schmutz continued pitching for Tacoma throughout the summer, but his transfer to Cincinnati at season's end seemed confirmed by widespread reports that Tacoma club owner George Shreeder had obtained $2,500 from Cincinnati for the rights to Schmutz.[30]

As it turned out, Shreeder decided that the Cincinnati offer was inadequate for a talent like Schmutz and held on to him for the 1912 season. Schmutz expressed his displeasure at this turn of events by returning his 1912 Tacoma contract unsigned.[31] He wanted out of Tacoma. But the reality of the reserve clause, and perhaps the sale of the Tacoma franchise to new owner Edd N. Watkins, compelled him to return to the Tigers.[32] The reunion would prove a disagreeable one, as the latest edition of the Tigers was dominated by untalented, often dissipated players who seemed to take pleasure in undermining the work of their staff ace. By mid-July, Tacoma was firmly entrenched in the NWL cellar, while Schmutz's individual record stood at a shuddering 2–14. Still, he remained held in high regard by NWL observers. A nationally circulated United Press wire report declared: "Schmutz is considered one of the best pitchers in the league, but despite his excellent work he has won two and lost 14 this season through the poor support given him. He was not liked by the loafing members of the team and they practically threw his games away. [Schmutz] is a clean living, hard working pitcher."[33] By then, club owner Watkins had seen enough, releasing underperforming malcontents Ody Abbott and Pete Morse, and trading Schmutz to the NWL rival Vancouver Bees for three players (including Jimmy Agnew). In announcing the moves, Watkins added, "I do not want the impression to get out that Schmutz was traded because he was breaking training rules. He is a man of the best habits and takes the greatest care of himself. While he is a great pitcher, he has not been winning for us and I believe that he will have a better chance to better himself with [Vancouver manager Bob] Brown."[34]

Truer words were rarely spoken. Once in a Vancouver uniform, Schmutz went on a winning tear, capturing his first nine decisions for the Bees. He finished the season with a combined 13–17 record and reestablished himself as a major-league prospect.[35] He was chosen by the Philadelphia Phillies in the late-season minor-league player draft, and directed to report to the club's training camp the following spring.[36]

Once again, Schmutz's hopes for a major-league chance were dashed, as he appears to have been given no shot to make the roster by the Phillies. Instead, he was returned to Vancouver, where he promptly resumed the excellent work of the previous campaign. By now, an improved, more fluid delivery had added some velocity to his fastball. But Schmutz still did not throw hard. Instead, he pitched to contact, relying on control and his spitball to get him out of tight spots.[37] For the 1913 season, that formula produced a 16–10 Schmutz record for the NWL pennant-winning Vancouver Bees, his selection to various NWL all-star teams, and, at long last, a legitimate shot at a major-league job. That July, Schmutz's contract was purchased by the National League Brooklyn Superbas, reportedly on the recommendation of retired fireballer Amos Rusie.[38] The $5,400 that Brooklyn club boss Charles Ebbets paid for Schmutz was high for an untested minor leaguer, but only a fraction of the $60,000 that Ebbets was prepared to lay out for new playing talent that summer.[39] New recruit Schmutz was to finish the NWL campaign with Vancouver, and then report to Brooklyn manager Bill Dahlen in September.[40] For reasons unclear, however, Schmutz remained in the Pacific Northwest that fall.

Prior to leaving his Seattle home for spring camp in February 1914, a grateful Schmutz sent Ebbets a letter. "I take the opportunity to state that the ambition of my life—the entering of the major leagues—has been realized," he wrote, "and I hope that I will be of as much service to you as I have been to [Vancouver manager] Brown. I have taken the best of care of myself this winter and am anxiously awaiting the opening of the training season."[41] Although Ebbets—feeling the competitive pressure applied by the new Brooklyn Tip-Tops of the upstart Federal League—had overstocked new manager Wilbert Robinson's pool of pitching candidates, Schmutz showed enough in spring exhibition play to survive the cut and make the Opening Day roster.

Once the regular season began, Schmutz saw no action for almost a month. He finally made his major-league debut on May 13, 1914, pitching a flawless inning with two strikeouts in relief of Bull Wagner in a 6–0 loss to Chicago. Two other scoreless relief outings followed. Then, after three weeks of inactivity, Robinson used Schmutz again: two innings of scoreless mop-up relief in a 6–0 defeat by St. Louis on June 13. Five days later, he got the call early, relieving starter Frank Allen in the top of the second inning with the Robins already trailing Cincinnati, 2–0.[42] From there, Schmutz pitched hitless ball until finally weakening in the ninth, when he gave up two runs on four hits to complete a 4–1 loss to the Reds.

After several more weeks of inaction, Schmutz was finally given a start—in an exhibition game against the Rochester Hustlers of the Class AA International League. He responded to the audition with a complete game, four-hit shutout, prompting the press back home to observe that "maybe after that showing fat Wilbert Robinson will give the Seattle lad a chance to work in a real league game."[43] But instead, Brooklyn brass assayed shipping Schmutz to its own IL farm club in Newark "in order that the tall lad from the Northwest will get the player preparation required for big leagues."[44] Armed with a guaranteed two-season contract—a benefit of Brooklyn's combat with the Federal League—Schmutz successfully resisted the effort to send him down and remained a member of the big club. On July 23, he got his first major-league start in an away game against the Cardinals. Schmutz surrendered a run in the bottom of the first, but thereafter held the opposition scoreless until he was removed in the top of the seventh for pinch-hitter Jack Dalton. A two-out Dalton single delivered Casey Stengel (Schmutz's road roommate) from third and gave Brooklyn a 2–1 lead. Unhappily for Schmutz, the Cardinals immediately pounced on reliever Ed Reulbach for three runs, leaving the first-time starter with a no-decision in the 4–2 loss.

Two subsequent starting assignments did not go as well. On August 6, Schmutz was yanked after a five-run first inning against St. Louis in a 7–2 loss. Two weeks later, he left after five innings trailing 4–0 in a 7–2 defeat by Cincinnati. A final start on September 11 produced a better effort, an 11-hit complete game in a

Schmutz posted a 1–3 record for the 1914 Brooklyn Robins.

3–0 loss to aging New York Giants pitching master Christy Mathewson. The defeat dropped Schmutz's record to 0–3. But with the 1914 season approaching an end, he finally registered a victory. Relieving starter Reulbach with the Robins trailing 2–0 in a September 25 home game against Pittsburgh, Schmutz was the beneficiary of shoddy late-inning fielding by the Pirates and emerged a 3–2 victor. Ordinarily a harmless batsman, Schmultz doubled in the ninth and scored the winning run himself on a throwing miscue by Pirates shortstop Wally Gerber. Days later, he made a substandard relief outing, giving up five runs in four innings and getting no decision in a 9–7 loss to the Phillies.

In 18 appearances for Brooklyn, Schmutz posted a 1–3 record with a 3.66 ERA in 59 innings. He struck out 23 and walked 14 while opposing batters batted .265 against him. Despite such mediocre numbers, the 23-year-old Schmutz had made a decent-enough rookie showing, and the youngster could be expected to improve under the tutelage of manager Robinson, an astute developer of pitching prospects. He'd have to, as the Robins had made considerable strides in team performance, improving on their 1913 season by 10 wins. Competition for spots on the 1915 club was likely to be brisk.

Despite unconfirmed reports of offseason bouts with shin splints and malaria, Schmutz reported to Brooklyn's spring camp in his customary excellent condition.[45] Once again, candidates for the pitching staff were plentiful, but Schmutz's cause was aided by arm miseries that put veteran hurlers Nat Rucker and Jack Coombs temporarily on the shelf. Soon, the preseason work of Schmutz and other youngsters drew the praise of Robinson. Following an exhibition game against Washington, Robbie declared, "In Schmutz, Appleton, Smith, and Dell, I have a quartet of young pitchers who will win a lot of games for me this summer."[46]

Schmutz was among the pitchers who made the expanded Opening Day roster, and was immediately sent into action in the inaugural game against the Giants. Entering the contest with Brooklyn already trailing, 7–0, he held Giants bats in check for three innings, but was then tattooed for four doubles and a single in a five-run sixth. Schmutz was relieved by Elmer Brown in the seventh—and would never appear in another major-league game. Several days thereafter, he was one of four pitchers sent to the minors as Brooklyn trimmed its roster to the 21-player limit.[47]

The remainder of the season was mostly grim for Schmutz. He was ineffective pitching for the International League Newark Indians, going 2–4 with a 6.29 RA in 73 innings pitched. He was then remanded back

to Brooklyn, which immediately optioned Schumtz to the Salt Lake City Bees of the Class AA Pacific Coast League.[48] He fared no better there. In eight games, he posted a 1–2 record with a 5.22 ERA in 29⅓ frames. As September approached and with Brooklyn's acquiescence, Salt Lake released Schmutz.[49] He was then signed by the hometown Seattle Giants of the Northwestern League, where he seemed to regain form pitching against Class B batters.[50] On September 16, a four-hit, 9–1 Schmutz victory over the Spokane Indians gave Seattle the NWL crown and ended a trying year on an upbeat note.[51]

During the offseason, Schmutz filed a grievance with the National Commission, the governing body of Organized Baseball, claiming that he had been underpaid for the 1915 season. Upon consideration, the commission agreed and awarded Schmutz $875, the difference between the salary specified in his binding two-year contract with Brooklyn and what he had been paid while pitching for Salt Lake and Seattle.[52] He then returned to the Seattle Giants and registered the most successful year of his professional career. He began the 1916 season by tossing 31 consecutive scoreless innings before a Seattle fielding miscue let in a run.[53] By season's end, Schmutz had posted a 19–11 (.633) record for a weak-hitting, next-to-last-place club that otherwise went 41–61 (.402). His 275 innings pitched demonstrated the soundness of his throwing arm, while his 106 strikeouts were a personal best.[54] Yet despite this sterling performance and Schmutz's youth (he was still only 25 years old), he went unclaimed in the postseason minor-league player draft, unwanted by either a major-league or higher minor-league club.

The rejection appears to have soured Schmutz on professional baseball. He refused to report to Seattle's spring camp in April 1917, prompting the club to sell him to Vancouver.[55] Schmutz would not report there, either. Instead, he signed as pitcher-manager of the Dry Docks, the club entered in the semipro Seattle Shipbuilders League by the Seattle Construction and Dry Dock Company."[56] When not in his baseball uniform, Schmutz was an electrician with the company.

The following winter, with the country fully engaged in World War I, Schmutz enlisted in the US Army. Initially stationed near home at Camp Lewis, he was soon playing ball for the juggernaut camp baseball team, coached by his friend and former Seattle High School teammate Charlie Mullen. In addition to Mullen and Schmutz, the Camp Lewis squad included former major-league hurlers Jim Scott and Duster Mails, while center field was patrolled by erstwhile Seattle High standout and St. Louis Cardinals prospect Ten Million.[57]

The Camp Lewis games came to an end, however, when the outfit was shipped to France in July 1918. But before leaving for the front, Schmutz became engaged to Brenda Jenkins, the 20-year-old daughter of a Seattle shipbuilding magnate.

A proud member of the 316 Sanitary Train of the 91st Infantry Division, Sergeant Charles Schmutz alternated duties on the battlefront with playing company baseball during lull periods in the fighting. Although the war-ending armistice was signed in November, his unit remained in France and did not leave for home until April 1919.[58] Shortly after his arrival back in Seattle, he and Brenda were married at the Jenkins family residence. Following a three-week honeymoon in the Canadian Rockies, the newlyweds set up housekeeping in a posh Seattle neighborhood, their newly built residence courtesy of the bride's wealthy father. In February 1920, the couple had their first child, a daughter named Nancy Low who, sadly, died shortly after birth. Some six years later, the arrival of daughter Nancy Brenda made the Schmutz family complete.

In early 1920, Schmutz joined the sales force at Graybar Electric, a Seattle wholesaler of electrical supplies and appliances. He would hold well-paying sales and executive positions at Graybar for the next 37 years. While Charlie worked and pitched on weekends for area semipro teams that often reunited him with his high school teammates, Brenda took to the Seattle social circuit.[59] Her attendance, usually in the company of her twin sister, Thelma Jenkins Anderson, and/or her socialite mother, Edith, at high-tone luncheons, art gallery exhibitions, and the like was regularly noted in the local press.[60]

The onset of the Great Depression appears to have had no effect on the Schmutzes. Charlie remained gainfully employed, while Brenda (usually with sister Thelma in tow) embarked on lengthy sojourns to Mexico, France, the Orient, and other faraway destinations, leaving the care of daughter Nancy to Charlie and the household domestic staff.[61] An unspecified illness, however, brought Brenda's gallivanting to a premature halt. She died at home on July 3, 1938, at the age of 39.

In 1940, Schmutz remarried, taking 34-year-old divorcee Dorene Young Dusky as his second wife.[62] The marriage was not a happy one, and the couple divorced five years later.[63] Now well into middle age, Schmutz, when not attending to work at Graybar Electric, immersed himself in baseball-related activities. He got deeply involved in Seattle youth baseball; played in area old-timers games; was appointed to the Seattle Rainiers Baseball Boosters Association; and

was a participant in regular reunions of the still locally celebrated Seattle High School team of 1907.[64] In addition, he was an active member of the American Legion and other Seattle civic organizations, and a renowned fisherman.

No one in Seattle was happier than Charlie Schmutz when the Brooklyn Dodgers won the 1955 World Series.[65] And four years later, he made the trip to Los Angeles to see his former club capture the 1959 world championship. By now, however, the infirmities of advancing age were closing in on Schmutz. He survived colon cancer surgery but was plagued by heart disease. On June 27, 1962, he suffered a heart attack while at home and was pronounced dead on arrival at Seattle's Providence Hospital.[66] Charles Otto Schmutz was 71, survived by his brother Ernest, sister Frances Schmutz Nelson, daughter Nancy Schmutz Hall, and four grandchildren.[67] Following services at a local funeral parlor, his remains were cremated and subsequently interred at the Washelli Columbarium at Evergreen-Washelli Memorial Park, Seattle, a far remove from the sunny Southern California city where the full and eventful life of Charlie Schmutz had begun more than seven decades earlier.[68] ■

Sources

Sources for biographical info include the Charlie Schmutz file with player questionnaire maintained at the Giamatti Research Center, National Baseball Hall of Fame and Museum, Cooperstown, New York; US Census data and Schmutz family posts accessed via Ancestry.com; and the articles cited in the endnotes. Unless otherwise noted, minor-league stats have been taken from Baseball-Reference, major-league data from Retrosheet.

Notes

1. Debuting with the Boston Red Sox in 1908, Deadball slugger Gavvy Cravath preceded Schmutz to the majors. But Cravath was born in San Diego County, not the city itself. Cravath's birthplace in Poway lies about 22 miles northeast of the San Diego city line.
2. Schmutz's paternal grandparents were Swiss immigrants who settled in Wisconsin. His siblings were brother Ernest (born 1894) and sister Frances (1911).
3. Ten (No Middle Name) Million later became a St. Louis Cardinals prospect until a knee injury ruined his playing career. See "St. Louis Cardinals Secure Ten Million," *Seattle Times*, January 13, 1912.
4. Evidently unsure of his chances of making the Seattle High team, Schmutz also organized a sandlot club called the Nationals to play other Puget Sound amateur nines. And even after he became the high school's star hurler, Schmutz pitched for the Nationals as well. "National Team Is Ready," *Seattle Times*, March 21, 1907.
5. Current baseball references list Schmutz's height as 6'1" or 6'1½." Some Deadball Era sources had him a bit taller, and the posthumous player questionnaire completed by his brother Ernest gave Schmutz's height as 6'3".
6. "Schmutz Wins for Seattle," *Seattle Times*, September 5, 1915.
7. "Dug's Team Stung by High School Bunch," *Seattle Times*, April 18, 1907.
8. "High School Beats Seattle; Schmutz Is Wizard," *Seattle Post-Intelligencer*, April 18, 1907.

9. The exhibition was Seattle's first World's Fair-type extravaganza, intended to advertise economic opportunity in the city and to promote Seattle as the gateway to Alaskan adventure and riches. The Seattle High School baseball tour eventually cost its sponsors almost $4,000.

10. "Western Was Easy," *Washington Herald*, July 7, 1907.

11. *Washington Times*, July 11, 1907.

12. Days after the Seattle High drubbing of Western, the hometown daily published a photo of the team in uniform. With the exception of Schmutz, none of the SHS players is physically large, and they indeed all look like teenagers. *Seattle Times*, July 17, 1907.

13. One Washington observer judged Agnew a "better box artist" than Schmutz, and Agnew would later pitch professionally, rising as high as the Pacific Coast League. *Washington Herald*, July 12, 1907.

14. For a detailed retrospective on the Seattle High tour of 1907, see David Eskenazi, "Wayback Machine: Seattle's First Ambassadors," Sportspress Northwest, October 18, 2011, http://sportspressnw.com/2122105/2011/wayback-machine-seattles-first-athletic-ambassadors; and Clark Squire, "Sizzling Schmutz," *Seattle Times*, April 23, 1956.

15. Since its opening in 1902, the school's official, but seldom-used, name was Washington High School. For some reason, local newspapers sometimes referred to Seattle High by its official name (Washington HS) during the 1908 baseball season. See e.g., "Washington High Team Gets Whitewashed," *Seattle Times*, April 8, 1908.

16. "Washington High Team Gets Whitewashed."

17. See e.g., "Websters Win Game from Clinton Stars," *Seattle Times*, September 28, 1908: "Schmutz had his spitball well tuned and struck out 15" during a 13-inning 1–0 Websters victory over the Clinton All-Stars. At the time, there was nothing remarkable about high schoolers like Schmutz playing semipro ball, and doing so did not jeopardize their high school eligibility. A photo of Schmutz, Jimmy Agnew, and a Tacoma High School catcher named Hanna in their Websters uniforms was published in the *Seattle Times*, July 19, 1908.

18. Widespread report that Schmutz had signed with the Northwestern League Tacoma Tigers proved erroneous.

19. "Fans Wake Up; Feel Satisfied," *Tacoma Ledger*, March 14, 1909.

20. Located in the city's Wallingford neighborhood, Lincoln High had opened in September 1907. It was one of several new institutions built to accommodate Seattle's exploding high school-age population.

21. "Lincoln Wins Championship," *Seattle Times*, June 5, 1909. Because Seattle High School was no longer the city's only public high school, the Board of Education decided to rename the institution Broadway High School. The new name took effect in Fall 1908, and was taken from the location of the erstwhile Seattle High School at Broadway and East Pine Street. For more on the confusing early-century name changes of Seattle's high schools, see "Seattle Public Schools, 1862-2000: Broadway High School," http://www.historylink.org/File/10475, posted September 4, 2013.

22. The Baseball-Reference entry for Charlie Schmutz (and high school teammate Charlie Mullen as well) currently lists him as having attended Seattle's Broadway High School. This is incorrect, as Schmutz was never a student at the institution during the years (1909–46) that it was called Broadway High. In his freshman and sophomore years (1906–08), Schmutz attended Seattle High School, while he spent his junior year (1908–09) at Lincoln High. Similarly, Mullen never attended Broadway HS. He was a June 1908 graduate of Seattle High School.

23. "Two Thrown into Lake When Canoe Capsizes," *Seattle Times*, June 21, 1909.

24. "Charley Schmutz Now Pitching in Montana," *Seattle Times*, July 11, 1909.

25. As recorded in the 1910 US Census, via Ancestry.com.

26. *Tacoma Ledger*, April 8, 1910. The malady was attributed to an unspecified wound that had become infected. During his time in Tacoma, Schmutz purportedly acquired the nickname "King" assigned to him

27. Schmutz's strikeout total is taken from the *1911 Reach Official Guide*, 374. His other stats come from Baseball-Reference.

28. It was subsequently reported that the 1911 season log of Schmutz and other Tacoma hurlers was brought down by the club's second-half disintegration. "Training Season Starts March 15," *Tacoma Ledger*, January 9, 1912.

29. "Miles Netzel Signs with Reds," *Seattle Times*, August 4, 1911.

30. "Three Beauties for $7,500," *Detroit Times*, October 6, 1911. The other Tacoma hurlers reportedly sold to Cincinnati were Fred Annis and Blaine Gordon. The three-pitcher sale was subsequently reiterated in news articles published in the *Sault Ste. Marie* (Michigan) *Evening News*, October 11, 1911; *Saginaw* (Michigan) *News*, October 13, 1911; (Springfield) *Illinois State Journal*, October 31, 1911; and elsewhere.

31. *Seattle Times*, January 18, 1912.

32. "Charley Schmutz Is Ready To Join Club," *Tacoma Ledger*, January 29, 1912.

33. "Loafers Released by Tacoma Mogul," (Portland) *Oregon Journal*, July 19, 1912, and elsewhere.

34. "Watkins Gives Team General Shaking Up," *Tacoma Ledger*, July 19, 1912. Agnew, meanwhile, was reluctant to take his old high school teammate's place on the Tacoma roster and refused to report. Tacoma eventually sold Agnew to the NWL Portland Colts, where he finished the season with a combined 14–12 record.

35. Final 1912 Northwestern League season stats, *Oregon Journal*, November 12, 1912. NWL stats in *Sporting Life*, November 2, 1912, put Schmutz's record at 12–15, but include fewer games (28 vs. 33) and fewer innings-pitched (254 vs. 261). Baseball-Reference has no 1912 numbers for Schmutz.

36. "Four Northwestern Players Who Report to Majors Next Season," *Oregon Journal*, September 29, 1912. A rival newspaper had earlier reported that Vancouver had sold the Schmutz contract to the Phillies in August. See *The* (Portland) *Oregonian*, August 6, 1912.

37. A Cincinnati Reds scout named O'Hara discounted Schmutz as a major-league prospect, saying he "has no fast ball. Charlie's main reliance is his spitball, slow ball, and excellent control.""Cincinnati Scout Picked Bob Ingersoll over Schmutz," *Seattle Times*, July 9, 1913.

38. "Dahlen May Have a 'Find,'" *New York Tribune*, November 2, 1913, and *Springfield* (Massachusetts) *Republican*, February 1, 1914. At the time, the down-on-his-luck Rusie was on the Tacoma Tigers groundskeeping crew.

39. "Dodgers To Pay Out $60,000 For Players," *Washington Evening Star*, 39 August 12, 1913, and "These Youngsters Go To Major Leagues Next Season," *Oregon Journal*, September 21, 1913. An earlier report that Schmutz had been sold to the Detroit Tigers proved false.

40. As reported in the *Kalamazoo* (Michigan) *Gazette*, *Philadelphia Inquirer*, and *Washington Evening Star*, July 22, 1913.

41. *New York Tribune*, February 1, 1914.

42. The Robins was the new and unofficial nickname bestowed upon the Brooklyn club in 1914 in tribute to popular new manager Wilbert Robinson.

43. "Schmutz Wins Shut-Out Game," *Seattle Times*, July 8, 1914.

44. Abe Yager, "The Superbas Revival," *Sporting Life*, July 11, 1914.

45. Unidentified 1914–15 newspaper articles cited in "Happy Birthday, Charlie Schmutz!" Mighty Casey Baseball, https://mightycaseybaseball.com/2018/01/02/happy-birthday-charlie-schmutz/, posted January 2, 2018; *Seattle Times*, September 3, 1915.

46. "Other Sport Comment," *Washington Herald*, April 9, 1915.

47. The others sent down were Raleigh Aitchison, Joe Chabek, and Elmer Brown.

48. "National League Notes," *Sporting Life*, July 24, 1915; *Washington Post*, July 7, 1915. By virtue of the two-year contract that he signed prior to the 1914 season, Schmutz remained Brooklyn property.

49. *Sporting Life*, August 28, 1915; Seattle Times, September 1, 1915.

50. "Schmutz returns," *Seattle Star*, September 3, 1915. "Schmutz will still be the property of Brooklyn but will finish the season here," the paper reported.

51. "Seattle Clinches 1915 Championship," *Tacoma Ledger*, September 17, 1915.

52. "Work of the National Commission," *Sporting Life*, March 11, 1916. See also, *Macon* (Georgia) *Telegraph* and *New Orleans States*, March 5, 1916.

53. *The Oregonian*, May 27, 1916.

54. Schmutz's 1916 strikeouts total comes from Northwestern League stats published in Sporting Life, January 13, 1917. Baseball-Reference has no strikeout data for the 1916 NWL season.

55. "Charles Schmutz Sold to Vancouver Club," *Tacoma Ledger*, April 18, 1917; "Schmutz Is a Beaver Now," *Tacoma Times*, April 18, 1917.

56. "Beavers Have High Hopes of Capturing Pennant This Year," *Seattle Times*, April 22, 1917.

57. *Daily Missoulian* (Montana), March 10, 1918, *Seattle Times*, March 17, 1918, *Tacoma Ledger*, April 10, 1918, and elsewhere; "St. Louis Cardinals Secure Ten Million," *Seattle Times*, January 13, 1912.

58. While awaiting embarkation at the French port of Saint-Nazaire, Schmutz had a happy reunion with another old friend/teammate, Sergeant Jimmy Agnew.

59. Among other things, Schmutz pitched for Charlie Mullen's Mount Vernon club, the 1920 winners of the semipro Big Six Skagit League, and hurled Auburn to the championship of the Valley League the following year. Later, he served as a commissioner (with former Seattle Siwashes boss Dan Dugdale) of the semipro Seattle Community League.

60. See e.g., "Social Notes," *Seattle Times*, November 1, 1927; March 18, 1928; February 10, 1931; March 8, 1933; June 29, 1934; and November 5, 1935.

61. See e.g., "Social Notes," *Seattle Times*, February 23, 1934; February 17, 1935; April 18, 1937.

62. Online state marriage records indicate that the couple was married in Clallam, Washington, on September 3, 1940.

63. "Vital Statistics/Divorce Granted," *Seattle Times*, October 26, 1945.

64. The Seattle Rainiers were a member of the Class AAA Pacific Coast league. During the late 1930s, Schmutz had been on the booster committee of the Seattle Indians, as the Rainiers were previously known.

65. Schmutz had offered a hesitant newspaper prediction of victory by his old club, while one-time Yankee Charlie Mullen confidently forecasted a New York win in the Series. See *Seattle Post-Intelligencer*, September 28, 1955.

66. Death certificate contained in the Charlie Schmutz file at the Giamatti Research Center. The immediate cause of death was listed as coronary occlusion due to auricular fibrillation.

67. "C. O. Schmutz, Former Major Leaguer, Dies," *Seattle Times*; "Charles O. Schmutz," *Seattle Post-Intelligencer*, June 28, 1962.

68. Posthumous player questionnaire completed by brother Ernie Schmutz and confirmed by Evergreen-Washelli Memorial Park staff to the writer via telephone, October 29, 2018.

American Indian Baseball in Old North County

San Diego Heritage at Riverside's Sherman Institute

Tom Willman

On May 3, 1905, much of California discovered that Native Americans really could play baseball. On that day the team from Sherman Institute, the three-year-old federal Indian boarding school in Riverside, played its first game against college competition. The result was startling. In 10 innings, playing in Los Angeles, Sherman beat USC, 7–4.

"Back East somewhere," the *Los Angeles Times* noted, "some scribe once said the Indians were a success as fielders, but could not bat. He was half right." As for the condescension that Indians couldn't really be expected to understand the inside game, the *Times* writer observed, "'Poor Lo' has been the subject of much misplaced sympathy."

The game seems to have gone unremarked in San Diego, which was too bad. In a real sense, it was a San Diego County story. Among those on the field for Sherman that spring day in 1905 were baseball coach (and star athlete) Joe Scholder, a Kumeyaay-Diegueño Indian from Mesa Grande, east of Escondido; left fielder Camillo Ardillo, from the relocated Cupeño home at Pala, east of Fallbrook; second baseman Sylvas Lubo, who drove in the first run against USC; Freddy Casero, who put on an acrobatic show at short and was, like Lubo, from the Cahuilla reservation, northeast of Pala; catcher Alex Tortes, who had three hits that day; and right-fielder Ignacio Guanche, who hit one out of the park in the fifth and drove in another run in the 10th to break USC's heart. Tortes and Guanche were both from the Santa Rosa reservation of Mountain Cahuilla.[2]

These reservations are strung like a necklace around the 6,000-foot landmark of Palomar Mountain in North County San Diego. They are one cluster among several dozen reservations and tribal lands sprinkled through the rugged chaparral backcountry of San Diego and Riverside counties. These are the tribes that formed Sherman Institute's original core population. When Sherman, new and untested, beat USC in 1905, it was a heady win. The victory helped mark Sherman as a showcase for Indian athletics.

The first three decades of the 20th century are generally viewed as the great age of the Native American athlete.[3] Much of that reputation rests on the well-publicized achievements of federal Indian boarding school athletes against top competition in the East and Midwest. Chief Bender and Jim Thorpe, both products of Carlisle Institute in Pennsylvania, are leading baseball examples. Sherman Institute, 25th and last in the chain of these Indian schools, provided similar exposure for top American Indian athletes of the West. It also provided a window on how ardently baseball was embraced across this "Mission Indian" country.

Until 1893, when Riverside County was created, all of this region was in San Diego County. The foundations of tradition were anchored here: the tribal homelands, the missions at San Diego and San Luis Rey (Oceanside), the *asistencia* (sub-mission) at Pala, and the fiefdoms of the land-grant ranchos.[4] But Sherman Institute, though farther north in Riverside, had a special claim to this North County heritage. The wife of Sherman's chief clerk, known simply as Mrs. Mitchell, lived quietly on campus, sometimes serving as matron in the girls' dormitory or cook in the dining hall.[5] It was a humble life of service for the former Estella Erolinda Estudillo. The landmark Estudillo Adobe in Old Town San Diego State Historic Park and the sprawling 35,500-acre Rancho San Jacinto Viejo were some of her family's lands.[6] Her brother, a frequent guest at Sherman, was Miguel Estudillo, Riverside's influential former state senator and longtime city attorney.[7] This notable San Diego association would serve Sherman Institute well for 38 years.[8]

That shared heritage was soon enhanced as Sherman and mighty Carlisle forged an unofficial bicoastal athletic circuit. There was a regular two-way flow of North County Indian students between the schools. Joe Scholder left his North County home to play football at Carlisle, then returned to coach at Sherman. Soon he was joined by the great Bemus Pierce (Seneca), who had been his Carlisle football captain. Both men would train generations of Sherman athletes before retiring in the 1940s. Meanwhile, over the years at least 75 Mission Indian students like Scholder would appear on the rolls at Carlisle.[9] More than a few were athletes.

Soon Sherman would earn its own national reputation in football and distance running. But it was baseball that would be Sherman's sport of greatest and most lasting importance. Baseball had been played in San Diego since the spring of 1871.[10] By the 1890s, the game was being played on North County reservations.[11] Some of these players would be with Sherman on May 20, 1905, when they met a touring team from Japan's Waseda University. The matchup drew a large crowd to Fiesta Park in Los Angeles.[12] Waseda won, 12–5, but several of its runs were unearned, and Sherman had the bases loaded when the game ended.[13] It had not been a mismatch. And it would pay a remarkable dividend. In September 1921, a team of former Sherman players sailed to Japan by special invitation to play a series of exhibition games with Japanese universities. Sherman baseball had been elevated to an instrument for diplomacy.[14]

As Sherman expanded its student population, a winning tradition was created. By the spring of 1907, Sherman was educating students from 48 distinct tribes.[15] The player pool deepened. There also were intramural squads representing the vocational shops, faculty-student games, and an alumni-student game at commencement festivities. At Sherman, baseball became a key part of the pan-Indian educational experience.

Baseball appealed to Native Americans on another level as well. The tribes and bands of San Diego and Riverside counties had their own history of abuse by the dominant culture. Broken treaties, usurped lands, lost water rights—all the familiar elements are part of this region's history. Reformer Helen Hunt Jackson's writings and popular 1884 novel *Ramona*, framing the Indians' plight, were researched and set in this landscape.[16] As recently as 1903, the Cupeño Indians of San Diego County had been forced from their traditional home at Warner's Hot Springs and compelled to relocate to Pala.[17] Yet life, and baseball, went on. Barely a year later, in the spring of 1904, the Pala Indian baseball team traveled to the coast to play Oceanside. Oceanside won, 14–13. "Both teams put up a good article of ball and the game was closely contested throughout," the *San Diego Evening Tribune* reported, adding of Pala rooters, "There was a large crowd present from San Luis Rey and the surrounding country."[18] Native Americans played baseball for fun; they turned out for excitement, for holiday diversion, even through complicated times. Certainly at Sherman, they also played for the fierce joy of showing people what they could do when the field was level. In the clash of cultures, baseball could be everyone's national pastime.[19]

Sherman's influence as a sustaining supporter and promoter of Native American baseball is clear. It's harder to imagine the spread of baseball as a popular recreation through a rural countryside, especially among insular reservations. But we get a glimpse of the dynamic through the testimony of the best-known Cahuilla player, Chief Meyers.

John Tortes Meyers was born in Riverside in 1880. His father was a Civil War veteran who died when Meyers was small. Meyers's mother was Cahuilla, and much of his youth was passed among her people. He spent some time in a small village called Spring Rancheria, near Mount Rubidoux and the fast-growing Riverside downtown. He also knew the traditional home of the Mountain Cahuilla, the Santa Rosa tribal lands on the flank of Mount San Jacinto, 60 miles to the east.

He was raised in a home where education was important—his mother was multilingual, his sister became a nurse—but this was before child labor laws. Meyers did not finish public school. Instead, he went to work in Riverside's groves and arbors, contributing to the family welfare. He would set out for the dusty mining leagues of Arizona and points east to seek his baseball fortune. Along the way he would spend a year at Dartmouth University, an association he prized all his life. But he would be going on 29 before he played in the majors, and it was those years spent living for the love of the game that would make him one of the National League's best hitters.

After the World Series of 1911, Meyers came home to Riverside. A local reporter caught him in a nostalgic moment, and Meyers recalled being a kid and admiring the team of G.D. Allen, who ran a sporting goods store in town. "He is the old original 33rd degree fan," Meyers said, "and when I was a mere kid years ago, I used to watch his team play and long for the time to come when I would be big enough to play on it.

Sherman Institute, the new federal Indian boarding school at Riverside, as it appeared in the popular national *Leslie's Weekly* in 1902.

Members of the 1914 Sherman Institute baseball team pose on the school lawn. The tall player at center holding the tip of the Sherman pennant is Emil Benson, Sherman's star pitcher that year. Benson threw a no-hitter against the University of Redlands.

The team was disbanded before I reached that age, but Mr. Allen has still retained his interest in baseball."[20]

In 1913, the Chicago White Sox came to Riverside for a spring training game against Sherman. The giddy crowd, estimated at 3,000, packed Evans Park to see Ed Walsh, Ray Schalk, Buck Weaver, Harry Lord, and Shano Collins. To the crowd's delight, the Sox turned it into a fun exhibition.[21] Final score: Chicago 14, Sherman 3.[22] But Sherman had its moments. Alum Saturnino Calac (Luiseño, Rincon band) was chosen Sherman's player of the game. He was busy and errorless at shortstop and blasted an exciting triple. Calac would go on to play Class D ball in California's State League and would return to coach at Sherman, where a regular parade of Calac clan athletes would enroll.

On March 14, 1914, Sherman defeated the University of Redlands, 3–1. Sherman's Emil Benson had 13 strikeouts and a no-hitter with no earned runs, according to Riverside coverage.[23] It was a symbolic triumph for Benson. On Sherman's rolls, his tribe was listed as "Digger."[24] This common demeaning term was an echo from the Gold Rush; it suggested lives of low subsistence, and it had justified generations of abuse, particularly against Central Californian Native Americans.[25] Benson (Mono) was from that country. But at Sherman, he also had the signature interests of a gifted student. That year he was involved in Sherman's Chautauqua-like literary societies, he was the editor of the *Sherman Bulletin*, and he would be the only boy in Sherman's small academic graduating class of 1914.[26] He was pitching for Riverside Poly High School in the spring of 1917 when America went to war. He dropped out to enlist in the Army.[27] He would pitch for the best teams at Camp Kearny, the sprawling "temporary camp" that popped up on the flats north of San Diego, before going overseas. Emil Benson would return as a sergeant and take up a long career as an Indian educator.

In those years, many former Sherman players found ways to go on living baseball lives. Lou Lockart (Pomo, Sherwood Valley Rancheria) had enrolled at Sherman in 1906. He had a hot fastball and a roundhouse curve and he quickly became Sherman's main pitcher. After two good years at Sherman, he bobbed up in many places. In 1910 he pitched for the Nebraska Indians. In 1911, he was at spring training in Murrieta with the Pacific Coast League Los Angeles Angels. He pitched decently in two games but was let go. Two months later he was reportedly pitching for an "all Japanese" touring team.[28] The winter of 1912 found him pitching for the Los Angeles Trainmen in the Beach League.[29] In 1918, rediscovered, he went to spring training with the Oakland Oaks of the PCL. In the third inning of an intersquad game he snapped a ligament in his pitching arm, ending his career.[30]

That same spring of 1918, a young pitcher named Chief Jamison was in camp with the Angels.[31] Bert Jamison (Seneca) had been a multisport athlete at Haskell, the Kansas Indian school, and there had met his wife, Sherman graduate Mary Golsh (Mission, Valley Center). In the Angels' camp, Jamison was wild, but his speed encouraged patience. Jamison was still with the Angels when the team discovered that Detroit Tigers great Sam Crawford was done with the majors and available. The Angels scooped Crawford up and Jamison was the last man cut when the squad broke camp.[32] Jamison would become a respected Sherman coach through the 1920s.[33]

Chief Meyers, in Butte, Montana, 1907, looking for his chance.

Of course, in 1918 everything changed. The civilian populace was drawn into the daily sacrifice of the war effort. Baseball seasons were cut short. Casualty counts mounted horrifically. On May 29, 1919, the *Sherman Bulletin* published a memorial page for nine former students who had died in France. One was Albert Ray, an Olympic-class runner. Three others had been ballplayers: Thomas Tucker, Alfonso Calac, and Phillip Calac. Among the many who served, another name is memorable in this context. Chief Meyers joined the US Marine Corps in the war's waning days. He did not see fighting. Meyers died in 1971. His grave marker bears no mention of baseball, only of his USMC service. He lies buried just upriver from the site of Spring Rancheria.[34]

Soon enough, Sherman would be overtaken by another game changer. As new high schools and colleges began to field teams, join leagues, and regulate competition, Sherman was odd-man-out when schedules were built. Under governance of the nascent California Interscholastic Federation Southern Section, Sherman would be stuck in freelance competition until 1939.[35]

And yet, today, after a century of evolution, Sherman—now fully accredited Sherman Indian High School—still exists as a Native American boarding school. It still occupies the same land where its cornerstone was laid in 1901. Its athletes still compete with high success, and on grounds that date to the Deadball Era. Its baseball teams still play with old-school panache. Sherman Indian High School stands as a living monument to the great age of the Native American athlete, and North County San Diego has had a lot to do with that. ■

Acknowledgments

Much of the research for this project, including a survey of bound volumes of the weekly *Sherman Bulletin* from 1907 to 1920, was done at the Sherman Indian Museum at Sherman Indian High School in Riverside, California. I wish to acknowledge the long-running hospitality, insightful guidance and assistance of the museum's curator, Lorene Sisquoc. The museum invites research inquiries. For more information, see http://www.shermanindian.org/museum.

A growing archive of Sherman images and documents is now available on the web, through a partnership with the Library of the University of California, Riverside. Visit Calisphere.org and find Sherman at "View All Statewide Partners."

I also wish to thank Ruth McCormick, local history specialist at the main Riverside Public Library, for her resourceful help and patience, and for sharing her passion for baseball history as well. For information about the Riverside Local History Resource Center, see https://www.riversideca.gov/library/history.asp.

The Cumberland County (Pennsylvania) Historical Society is keeper of the rich online historical archive of Carlisle Indian School, including digital images, student publications, records and manuscripts. For more about their research opportunities, see https://carlisleindian.historicalsociety.com.

Notes

1. "Indians Play Baseball Too," *Los Angeles Times*, May 4, 1905.
2. Sherman Institute student registration log books, Sherman Indian Museum, Riverside, California.
3. Joseph B. Oxendine, *American Indian Sports Heritage* (Champaign, IL: Human Kinetics Books, 1988), 239.
4. Richard L. Carrico, *Strangers in a Stolen Land: Indians of San Diego County From Prehistory to the New Deal* (San Diego: Sunbelt Publications, 2008), 135 et seq.
5. "Staff Changes at Sherman Institute Made Known," *Riverside Daily Press*, July 31, 1940.
6. "La Casa de Estudillo," California Department of Parks and Recreation, https://www.parks.ca.gov/?page_id=28012.
7. Elmer Wallace Holmes, *History of Riverside County California; with Biographical Sketches; Hon. Miguel Estudillo* (Los Angeles: Historic Record Company, 1912) 344–8.
8. *Riverside Enterprise*, November 8, 1919; "Staff Changes at Sherman Institute Made Known," *Riverside Daily Press*, July 31, 1940.
9. "Carlisle Indian School History: Mission," Cumberland County Historical Society, https://carlisleindian.historicalsociety.com/mission/.
10. Bill Swank, The San Diego Historical Society, *Baseball in San Diego: From the Plaza to the Padres* (San Francisco: Arcadia Publishing, 2005), 11.
11. Swank, 126.
12. "A New Departure: An Epoch-Marking Game of Base Ball," *Sporting Life*, June 10, 1905.
13. "Wiry Japs Wallop Reds," *Los Angeles Times*, May 21, 1905.
14. "Sherman Team Goes to Japan to Play Ball," *Arlington Times*, September 16, 1921.

15. "General News," *Sherman Bulletin*, March 6, 1907.

16. Clifford E. Trafzer, Matthew Sakiestewa Gilbert, and Lorene Sisquoc, eds. *The Indian School on Magnolia Avenue: Voices and Images From Sherman Institute* (Corvallis, OR: Oregon State University Press, 2012) 45–7.

17. Carrico, *Strangers in a Stolen Land*, 155.

18. *San Diego Evening Tribune*, May 23, 1904.

19. John Bloom, *To Show What an Indian Can Do: Sports at Native American Boarding Schools* (Minneapolis: University of Minnesota Press, 2000) XVI–XX; Trafzer, Gilbert, and Sisquoc, eds., The Indian School on Magnolia Avenue 6, 27–8.

20. "Meyers is Home After Big Games," *Riverside Daily Press*, November 6, 1911.

21. "White Sox Defeat Redskins, 14 to 3," *Chicago Inter Ocean*, March 26, 1913.

22. "Play Y.M.C.A. Benefit Ball Game: The Largest Crowd In The History of Riverside's Big Ball Park See The Chicago White Sox Defeat Sherman," *Sherman Bulletin*, March 26, 1913.

23. "Riverside Wins in Three Games," *Riverside Daily Press*, March 16, 1914.

24. Sherman Institute student registration logbooks: Emil Benson, original enrollment October 19, 1911.

25. Allan Lönnberg, "The Digger Indian Stereotype in California," *Journal of California and Great Basin Anthropology* 3, No. 2, UC Merced, 1981. https://escholarship.org/uc/item/6qq09790.

26. "Graduating Class of Sherman Institute," *Riverside Daily Press*, March 15, 1914.

27. Emil Benson World War I service dates, in the U.S. Department of Veterans Affairs BIRLS Death File, 1850–2010, (Provo, Utah). Accessed at ancestry.com.

28. "Japanese Baseball Star Proves to be an Indian," *Los Angeles Times*, May 11, 1911.

29. "School Sports," *Sherman Bulletin*, November 13, 1912.

30. "At the Training Camps," *Los Angeles Times*, March 16, 1918.

31. "At the Training Camps."

32. "Tigers Brace Up and Win," *Los Angeles Times*, March 29, 1918.

33. "Sherman Indians Play Ring Around the Rosy with Yuma Braves: Roll Up a Score of 75 Points in Championship Grid Battle," *Riverside Daily Press*, January 2, 1923.

34. Chief Meyers is buried at Green Acres Memorial Park in Bloomington, California.

35. Dr. John S. Dahlen, "Sherman Indian High School," CIF Southern Section, https://cifss.org/wp-content/uploads/2015/06/CIFSS-History-31-Sherman-Indian-School.pdf.

No. 19, Ted Williams, LF, San Diego Padres

Tom Larwin

It was June 1936 and a 17-year-old San Diego high school student signed his first professional baseball contract—with his parents' approval—to play for his hometown San Diego Padres. Ted Williams was "the kid," and he went on to play 42 games that summer for the Pacific Coast League Padres, ending the season as the team's regular left fielder. Williams graduated from high school in January and continued to play with the Padres in 1937.

In January 1933, Williams had started high school at Herbert Hoover—the Hoover Cardinals—a relatively new school in San Diego. By his junior year in 1935, he was primarily a pitcher for the Hoover High baseball team. Williams was already beginning to get public notice in the local news for his pitching and his hitting. He had attracted the interest of major-league baseball scouts, too, such as Herb Benninghoven of the St. Louis Cardinals and "Vinegar" Bill Essick of the New York Yankees.[1]

Williams's final season with the Hoover Cardinals, 1936, was characterized by superb pitching performances but also explosive hitting. He finished with a 10–2 record and four games with 13 or more strikeouts, once reaching 19.[2] But, in a sign of times to come, the April 13, 1936, *San Diego Union* featured a large photo of Williams swinging a bat under the headline "They'll Be Calling Him Bambino."[3]

1936: WILLIAMS'S FIRST PRO SEASON

Williams's high school playing career concluded at the end of May 1936, but he would remain a high school senior until January 1937, when he was due to graduate. With his high school career over, speculation ramped up, beginning on June 1 with an article that announced: "San Diego Contract Offered Williams."[4] It wasn't the Yankees or the Cardinals. It was San Diego! The team was in its first season in town, having moved south from Hollywood the previous winter. The article indicated that owner Bill Lane had offered a contract to Williams on May 30.

Finally, on June 27, the *Union* pronounced: "Williams, Former Hoover Star, Signed by Padres as Outfielder." The story noted that Williams had been a pitcher in high school, but would be used in the

Ted Williams, top row, second from right.

outfield because of his hitting ability. The terms of the contract kept Williams with the Padres for the remainder of 1936 without being farmed out.[5]

That day, June 27, Williams made his professional debut as a pinch-hitter in the second inning of a game against Sacramento. He was quickly struck out by Solons pitcher Cotton Pippen.[6]

On July 3, Williams entered his second professional game, again as a pinch-hitter. Behind 12–3 in the top of the seventh inning, manager Frank Shellenback called on Williams. He faced Los Angeles Angels pitcher Glen Gabler and singled, his first hit in professional baseball. Williams stayed in the game—not in the outfield but on the mound! He had modest success in his first inning but gave way after allowing a pair of home runs. That would be his only experience pitching for the Padres.

Williams got into 10 more games in July, mostly as a pinch-hitter. In his first five weeks in professional ball his batting average was .190.

August was a bit better for Williams. He started seven games and batted .250 for the month. He managed to pick up his first extra-base hits in an August 9 doubleheader against the Portland Beavers when he went 3-for-7 with a pair of doubles.

August also found Boston Red Sox general manager Eddie Collins visiting to watch the Padres, primarily to take a better look at second baseman Bobby Doerr. While there, Collins reportedly inquired "about the kid in right, that youngster Williams, whose swing looked good and who seemed able to drive in runs." He left with a handshake agreement with Padres owner Lane that the team would not trade Williams to anyone else without first consulting with Collins.[7]

September started with a stunning development for the Padres: the sudden departure of left fielder Chick Shiver to take a football coaching position. The loss of Shiver, who was red-hot through August, seemed like a knockdown blow to the Padres, who were within two games of first place. Manager Shellenback replaced him with Williams to start in left field for the rest of the season.

On September 1, two days after Williams turned 18, "The Kid" started in left against Sacramento. He was beginning to receive more media attention, too. For example, a photograph of Williams swinging a bat and titled "Public Enemy No. 1 to Floundering Sacs" was featured in the September 7 *Union*.

The press attention was not limited to San Diego. A fan wrote to a *Los Angeles Times* reporter and offered a bold—but very accurate, as it turned out— prediction concerning a "kid" playing for the Padres

"The Kid" as a San Diego Padre.

who was "tall, skinny, and awkward as hell" and "exceedingly nervous."[8] The fan concluded with a recommendation to "write a piece about this Williams and in a year you can look back and say 'I was the first baseball writer to predict that he would go places.'"

Williams started each of the team's 17 games in September and batted .305 for the month as the Padres won 11 of 17 to finish the season in second place, a game and a half behind Portland and tied with the Oakland Oaks.

The playoffs began on September 15. In best-of-seven series, the Padres were scheduled to play the Oaks while first-place Portland went up against the fourth-place Seattle Indians. Things did not go well for the Padres. They lost the Series, 4–1. Notably, Williams hit his first home run as a professional off Wee Willie Ludolph in Game One, a 6–3 loss.

Later that autumn, Williams received his first notice in *The Sporting News*; it came in the November 26 edition, in an article by Earl Keller under the headline "San Diego Counting Strongly on Young Home-Town Player."[9] After 42 minor-league games and 108 at-bats, "The Kid" was beginning to receive national attention.

The offseason for Williams was mainly devoted to high school. He graduated in January 1937 and received honors for outstanding performance in baseball…and in typing.[10] As spring training approached, Williams was a minor holdout for the 1937 season. However, by mid-March, it was reported that he had signed for a "nice raise" in salary.[11]

1937: WILLIAMS'S SECOND SEASON

On March 31, 1937, three days before the start of the season, it was reported that Williams was nursing a slight "charley horse."[12] The ailment would bother him for the first two months of the season. Williams said later that he had hurt his leg running on wet grass.[13]

His first 1937 start was in left field on April 11, 10 games into the season. He had been 1-for-9 in limited appearances. Batting seventh in the lineup, he managed to go 1-for-3, with the hit being Williams's first regular-season home run, driving in two runs in a 4–0 win.

Williams ended April by starting in eight consecutive games. He finished the month with two home runs, 13 RBIs, and a .260 batting average. His big game occurred on April 27, when he hit his second home run and drove in five runs. In a photo at the top of its sports page, the San Diego Evening Tribune captured the home run at the end of Williams's swing. It was a photo that would be used on the cover of Padres scorecards for a decade, between 1947 and 1957.[14]

He started 11 of the Padres' next 50 games. It could have been the charley horse that limited his playing time, but also there were mentions in the news about fielding lapses. Keller wrote that "Ted must get it in his head that fielding is just as important as hitting."[15] He ended May with his batting average at .226, having added no home runs and only three RBIs during the month.

Entering June, Williams was still mostly riding the bench and pinch-hitting. One exception was a June 6 doubleheader in which he played both games and went 5-for-8. Bill Swank, in his coverage of the 1937 Padres, wondered whether Shellenback had deliberately held Williams out, perhaps to teach him a lesson following his occasional defensive lapses.[16]

On June 19, Williams was again in the starting lineup. However, he was elevated in the order, batting fifth, and as June continued he would play all but one day to finish out the month. He went on to play in 96 of the remaining 99 games, starting 92 of them. For these 96 games he batted .298 with 21 home runs and 73 RBIs.

Coincidentally, a win on June 19 was the start of an eight-game win streak for the Padres. They had been in third place most of the season, but by early July the Padres had moved into first place.

"The Kid" had a two-home run game on July 13 and ended the month with midseason totals of 12 home runs and 64 RBIs.

The team sputtered a bit in August, going 16–15 for the month but ending it only 1½ games out of first. Williams had another productive month, batting .300 with six home runs and 16 RBIs. His season batting average had increased to .285. Through the entire month, the Padres were either in first place or within two games of it.

Having just turned 19, Williams started September with his second two-homer game in a Padres win on September 1. Another win on September 2 had San Diego back in first place. But the Padres went on a seven-game losing streak and September 12 found them five games out of first. Williams kept hitting, finishing the month with five home runs and 16 RBIs. Unfortunately, the team struggled, losing five of seven to the last-place Mission Reds in the last week of the season. They finished in third place, 5½ games behind Sacramento and one game behind the San Francisco Seals.

The regular season ended on September 19 with a doubleheader against the Reds. The Padres lost both games, but in the nightcap, Williams hit his 23rd home run in what would be his last at-bat for the San Diego Padres in a regular-season game.

Two days after the regular season ended, the Padres met Sacramento for a best-of-seven series. The winner would play the winner of the San Francisco-Portland matchup.

The team's September blues were reversed in the playoffs. The Padres swept the Solons. The Beavers did likewise to the Seals, so it was San Diego vs. Portland for the PCL championship.

It was no contest. The Padres swept the series. San Diego got hot at the right time

With a tight grip on two bats, a teenaged yet serious Ted Williams looks on.

in September (and one game in October) sweeping all eight of their playoff games.

In the team's second year in San Diego, 1937, the Padres were crowned PCL champions!

THE FOUNDATION FOR A HALL OF FAME CAREER

The Padres' first two years playing in San Diego produced two winning teams, finishing tied for second in 1936 and third in 1937. They made the playoffs both years and were crowned champions in '37.

What appeared to be a sidelight at the time was the emergence of a 17-year-old high school player—a hometown boy. That "The Kid" became one of the best players in the history of baseball meant that sidelight became the story.

As 1937 ended, Ted Williams was on his way—after a stop in Minneapolis for a final minor-league season—to a long career with the American League's Boston Red Sox. He had been on the radar of major-league scouts since he was 16 years old, and, as it turned out, by the time he was 20 Williams would be playing in the outfield for the Red Sox.

In conclusion, there are some remarkable aspects and coincidences associated with Williams and his two years as a San Diego Padre:

- He wore uniform number 19 as a Padre—the same number worn by another San Diego Padres icon and Hall of Famer, Tony Gwynn.

- In 1936, he played with another future Hall of Famer, Bobby Doerr, who would also be a teammate with the Red Sox. Doerr and Williams being teammates in 1936 is one of the rare times when two future Hall of Famers played on the same minor-league team.

- He hit a home run in his last regular season at-bat with the Padres in 1937—just as he would with the Red Sox in 1960.

- Finally, he pitched one game in relief for the Padres, in 1936, and he did the same for the Sox, taking the mound once in 1940. ■

TED WILLIAMS BATTING: SAN DIEGO PADRES 1936–1937

Year	Team	League	Pos	G	AB	R	H	2B	3B	HR	RBI	SB	AVG
1936	San Diego	PCL	of-p	42	108	18	29	9	2	0	11	2	.269
1937	San Diego	PCL	of	138	454	66	132	24	2	23	96	1	.291
	Totals			180	562	84	161	33	4	23	107	3	.286

NOTE: These statistics are based on a game-by-game summary for each season and include revised numbers from those commonly reported (e.g., 1938 *Spalding Official Base Ball Guide*). Specifically, in 1936 Williams had one more at-bat and one more double, resulting in a batting average of .269 for the season (as opposed to .271). For 1937, 96 RBIs were found as opposed to 98.

TED WILLIAMS POSTSEASON BATTING: SAN DIEGO PADRES 1936–1937

Year	Team	League	Pos	G	AB	R	H	2B	3B	HR	RBI	SB	AVG
1936	San Diego	PCL	of	5	16	4	3	0	0	1	3	0	.188
1937	San Diego	PCL	of	8	33	5	11	2	1	1	3	0	.333
Totals				13	49	9	14	2	1	2	6	0	.286

TED WILLIAMS PITCHING: MAJOR AND MINOR LEAGUE CAREER

Year	Team	League	G	GS	CG	ShO	SV	W	L	PCT	IP	H	R	ER	K	BB	ERA
1936	San Diego	PCL	1	0	0	0	0	0	0	.000	1.3	2	2	2	0	1	13.50
1940	Boston	AL	1	0	0	0	0	0	0	.000	2	3	1	1	1	0	4.50

Acknowledgments

There are two references that directly relate to the subject of this article and provided much of its research basis.

Tom Larwin, et al. *San Diego's First Padres and "The Kid": The story of the Remarkable 1936 San Diego Padres and Ted Williams' Professional Baseball Debut*. San Diego: Montezuma Press, 2019.

Bill Nowlin, ed. *The Kid: Ted Williams in San Diego*. Cambridge, MA: Rounder Books, 2005. In particular: Nowlin, "Ted Williams at Hoover High," 34–109; Dan Boyle, "The Splendid Splinter's 1936 PCL Debut: Who Is This Kid?," 120–27; Bill Swank, "Ted Williams, Earl Keller & the 1937 San Diego Padres," 128–59.

Notes

1. Ted Williams and John Underwood, *My Turn at Bat, The Story of My Life* (New York: Simon & Shuster, 1988), 36; John Updike, *Hub Fans Bid Kid Adieu, John Updike on Ted Williams* (London: Penguin, 2010), 6; Arthur Mann, "Baseball's Bad Boy," *Liberty*, May 9, 1940.
2. Tom Larwin, "Ted Williams Game Summaries, 1934–1938: High School, American Legion, and Area Leagues," in *The Kid: Ted Williams in San Diego*, ed. Bill Nowlin (Cambridge MA: Rounder Books, 2005), 112.
3. "They'll Be Calling Him Bambino," *San Diego Union*, April 13, 1936.
4. "San Diego Contract Offered Williams," *San Diego Evening Tribune*, June 1, 1936.
5. Ted Steinmann, "Williams, Former Hoover Star, Signed by Padres as Outfielder," *San Diego Union*, June 27, 1936.
6. With the Red Sox, Williams would face Pippen again. In his fourth game as a major leaguer on April 23, 1939, Williams faced Pippen (then with the Philadelphia A's) and went 2-for-2 with a single and a double. In all, in 1939 and 1940, Williams faced Pippen nine times in five games. He reached base six of those nine at-bats, with four hits and two walks, for a batting average of .571. Of Williams's four hits against Pippen, two were doubles and one was a home run.
7. Michael Siedel, *Ted Williams: A Baseball Life* (Chicago: Contemporary Books, 1991), 20.
8. Bob Ray, "The Sports X-Ray," *Los Angeles Times*, September 9, 1936.
9. Earl Keller, "San Diego Counting Strongly on Young Home-Town Player," *The Sporting News*, November 26, 1936.
10. Keller, *San Diego Evening Tribune*, February 4, 1937.
11. *Los Angeles Times*, March 25, 1937.
12. Keller, *San Diego Evening Tribune*, March 31, 1937.
13. Dick Hackenberg, *The Minneapolis Star*, March 29, 1938, 16.
14. Bill Swank, "Ted Williams, Earl Keller & the 1937 San Diego Padres," in *The Kid: Ted Williams in San Diego*, 142.
15. Keller, *San Diego Evening Tribune*, May 4, 1937.
16. Swank, "Ted Williams, Earl Keller & the 1937 San Diego Padres," 146.

Researching Ted Williams's Latino Roots

Bill Nowlin

There was one sentence that I read in Ted Williams's autobiography, *My Turn At Bat*, which set me off on a personal research journey that took me to some unexpected places and raised a few eyebrows along the way. It was a 44-word sentence about his mother, which I really only focused on the third time I read the book:

> Her maiden name was Venzer, she was part Mexican and part French, and that's fate for you; if I had had my mother's name, there is no doubt I would have run into problems in those days, the prejudices people had in Southern California.[1]

I was re-reading his autobiography while trying to organize material for the 1997 Masters Press book that I co-authored with Jim Prime: *Ted Williams, A Tribute.* I hadn't read *My Turn At Bat* for maybe 10 or 15 years,

but the sentence probably caught my eye that time around because early in the 1990s I had married a woman of Mexican-American ancestry. I wanted to find out more about May Williams's family background, but her surname was misspelled in Ted's book (Venzer for Venzor) which stymied further research.

After Jim's and my book came out, we heard from one of Ted's nephews, Manuel Herrera. He was a treasure trove of family lore and put me in touch with Sarah Diaz of Santa Barbara. She was May's sister—Ted's aunt. She was 94 years old at the time, but very sharp. Talking with both Manny and Aunt Sarah, I was able to put together a kind of family tree. Both of Ted Williams's maternal grandparents had come to the United States from Valle de Allende, Chihuahua, Mexico. Pablo Venzor and Natalia Hernandez Venzor entered the US at El Paso around 1890. May Venzor was born in El Paso in 1891. The family ultimately made its way to Santa Barbara.

May met her future husband, Sam Williams, in the Salvation Army. They made their home in San Diego.

One of May's brothers, Saul Venzor, was an accomplished baseball pitcher in Santa Barbara. When I learned the names of Ted's uncles and aunts, I dug into more research. In Saul Venzor's case, his 1963 obituary in the *Santa Barbara News-Press* said that he had given Ted Williams's his first baseball lessons and that Ted had told friends that "Mr. Venzor was his first instructor."[2]

While I was accumulating more information about Ted's family background—on both sides of the family—I had the opportunity to have lunch with Ted at his Florida home in April 2000. I asked him about Uncle Saul. He said, "He was my mother's brother… He was a pretty good baseball player. Santa Barbara. I don't know any other relatives that had much ability."[3]

And then he changed the subject. It didn't feel awkward, but it was clearly something he preferred not to talk about. As Ted himself had written in *My Turn at Bat* of growing up in San Diego in the 1930s, he was well aware of the racial prejudice he would have faced, with "no doubt" about it.[4] As Al Cassidy,

Three of Ted Williams's uncles with his grandmother Natalia Hernandez in Santa Barbara, ca. 1954. (L to R) Pete Venzor, Saul Venzor, Natalia Hernandez, Paul Venzor.

MAY WILLIAMS COLLECTION

the executor of Ted Williams's estate, told writer Ben Bradlee about Ted's early days, "Ted didn't want anyone to know he was part Mexican. It concerned him. He was afraid they wouldn't let him play. He'd say, 'It was an entirely different time back then.'"[5]

Over time, I visited San Diego, Santa Barbara, and Ted's uncle Ernesto Ponce in El Paso. I kept gathering information and then wrote an article for the *Boston Globe Magazine*. The article was published on June 2, 2002. That Ted Williams could be considered Hispanic came as a total surprise to those who never guessed the "Williams" surname might have masked another

element of his ethnicity. It was the first time the story had been explained.[6]

After his death, I helped organize three celebrations of Ted Williams's life during 2002–03, first at the Boston Public Library, then at the National Baseball Hall of Fame and Museum, and lastly (working with the local SABR chapter) at the San Diego Hall of Champions. I had met Sam and John Theodore "Ted" Williams (sons of the Hall of Famer's brother Danny) during a memorial event at Fenway Park in 2002. I invited the many relatives I had called or visited, and 33 relatives from Ted Williams's extended family attended the celebration at San Diego's Balboa Park at the Hall of Champions. Their surnames exemplified their own Latino background—names such as Amidon, Contreras, Mata, Ortiz, Ronquillo, and Venzor. There's a photograph of them all, which first ran in *The Kid: Ted Williams in San Diego* (Rounder Books, 2005) a joint project of nine SABR authors.[7]

In July 2010, nephew Ted Williams and I both took a trip to Mexico. Ricardo Urquidi Espinoza had invited me to come to speak at two different events: an evening gathering of sportswriters in the city of Chihuahua itself and then at a "Conferencia Historica" on the Patio Central de la Presidencia Municipal on July 10, 2010, in the city of Hidalgo del Parral. I invited Ted along. We also took in a baseball game in Parral, and made a side trip to the village of Valle de Allende. We met with local genealogists and historians there, and a couple of Venzors, too. My further research was eventually gathered into the book *Ted Williams: First Latino in the Baseball Hall of Fame*.

The book provokes debate over whether Ted Williams can be considered Latino, given that he apparently lived and identified as Anglo. Scholar Adrian

MAY WILLIAMS COLLECTION

Ted, May, and Danny Williams, ca. 1921.

Members of Ted Williams's extended family in Balboa Park, where they gathered during the celebration of his life at the San Diego Hall of Champions.

(L to R) Peggy Amidon, Judi (Amidon) Vista, Linda Amidon (Jim's wife), Louie Mata, Louie Mata III, Mari Mata, Mitchell Amidon (Jim's son), Virginia Amidon, Jackie Mata, Bill Amidon, Suzy Amidon, James Amidon, Ron Amidon, Nicholas Atondo, David C. Allen, Frank Venzor, Alyse Amidon, Dee (Venzor) Allen, Gero Lucero, Erich Venzor, Hugo Nathan Gaytan, Gudrun Venzor, David Ronquillo, Chaz Venzor, Ted Williams, Rose (Venzor) Larson, Karma Barber Arnold, Bob Larson, Teresa (Cordero) Contreras, Carrie (Venzor) Ortiz, unknown, Carol Jean Contreras.

PHOTO COURTESY OF BILL NOWLIN

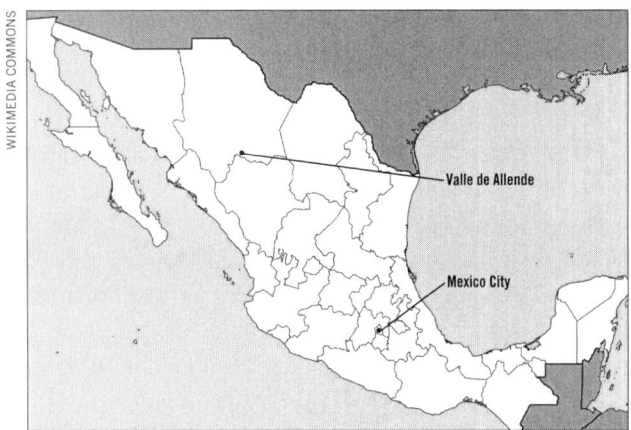

Valle de Allende is a small community of around 4,000 residents.

Burgos Jr. argues that it is "important that we do not rewrite the history of Latinos and baseball by retroactively inserting Williams." Burgos writes that Ted Williams should not be considered as Latino because he "did not identify as Latino nor was he racialized as such during his legendary career."[8] This seems to be the stance of Major League Baseball as well, who left Ted off a ballot of 60 "Latino Legends" in 2005.[9] Nonetheless, Ted Williams's previously unsung background has subsequently been incorporated into scholarship about him. (Ben Bradlee Jr. even mentioned my work in his 856-page tome, *The Kid*. He wrote, "No reporter...dug into [Ted Williams's] Mexican heritage until Bill Nowlin explored some of the Venzor family lineage in an article for the *Boston Globe Magazine*."[10]) Although Ted might have habitually brushed the subject of his heritage aside, researchers no longer can. ■

Notes

1. Ted Williams with John Underwood, *My Turn at Bat* (New York: Fireside, 1966, 1988), 28.
2. *Santa Barbara News-Press*, August 16, 1963.
3. Author interview with Ted Williams on April 28, 2000.
4. *My Turn at Bat*, 28.
5. Ben Bradlee Jr. interview with Al Cassidy, December 5, 2002. See Ben Bradlee, Jr., *The Kid: The Immortal Life of Ted Williams* (New York: Little, Brown and Company, 2013), 6.
6. Bill Nowlin, "El Splinter Esplendido, Ted Williams's Latino Heritage," *Boston Globe Magazine*, June 2, 2002.
7. *The Kid: Ted Williams in San Diego*, ed. Bill Nowlin (Cambridge, Massachusetts: Rounder Books, 2005). Contributing SABR authors were Carlos Bauer, Dan Boyle, Tom Larwin, Joe Naiman, Bill Swank, James D. Smith III, Stew Thornley, and G. Jay Walker.
8. Adrian Burgos, Jr., "No, Ted Williams Was Not Baseball's First Latino Superstar," *The Sporting News*, June 24, 2015.
9. Richard Sandomir, "Who's a Latino Baseball Legend?" *The New York Times*, August 26, 2005. https://www.nytimes.com/2005/08/26/sports/baseball/whos-a-latino-baseball-legend.html.
10. Ben Bradlee, Jr., *The Kid*, 27, 28.

The Longest No-Hitter in San Diego Padres History

Dick Ward's 1938 Extra-Inning Masterpiece

Gordon J. Gattie

Nearly 300 no-hitters have been thrown in the major leagues since 1876, but none of them have been thrown by a San Diego Padre. The closest any Padres pitcher has come to pitching immortality since San Diego joined the National League was on July 18, 1972, when Steve Arlin pitched 8⅔ hitless innings against the Philadelphia Phillies before Denny Doyle singled to left field.[1] However, many Padres fans believe the major-league franchise's best chance at a no-hitter happened on July 21, 1970, when Clay Kirby fired eight no-hit innings against the New York Mets before he was lifted for a pinch-hitter in the bottom of the eighth.[2]

Long before the Padres' major-league no-hit shortcomings, though, Dick Ward, pitching for the Pacific Coast League's San Diego Padres, threw 12⅔ innings of no-hit ball during a 16-inning 1–0 marathon victory over the Los Angeles Angels on August 30, 1938. Ward earned the complete-game shutout, allowing two hits and four walks while striking out three.[3] Even though Los Angeles managed two base hits during extra innings, Ward allowed no hits through the first nine innings, satisfying the PCL's definition for a no-hitter.[4]

Dick Ward was a journeyman minor-league pitcher playing in his seventh season of organized baseball when he threw his 16-inning shutout. He debuted professionally as a 23-year-old with the Wichita Aviators of the Western League during the 1932 season, and later that year advanced to the Angels in the PCL. The Angels were retooling for the 1932 season, transitioning from an independent minor-league club to a Chicago Cubs affiliate, and they needed to rebuild their pitching staff. Ward was among the rookie hurlers fighting for a rotation spot.[5] Following a slow spring, he started the season in Wichita and was recalled to Los Angeles in August.[6] There he compiled a 4–3 record and 4.87 ERA over 61 innings during his first experience in the Pacific Coast League.[7] Ward won 25 games for Los Angeles the following year, finishing second on the ballclub in wins, second in ERA (3.25), and third in innings pitched (285). He returned to the

Angels in 1934 though he made his major-league debut for the Cubs on May 3, pitching a scoreless ninth inning against the Boston Braves. Ward pitched in two more games before returning to Los Angeles. On November 21, 1934, he was traded to the St. Louis Cardinals with pitcher Bud Tinning for pitcher Tex Carleton; the Cardinals hoped Ward would translate his PCL success into wins at the big-league level.[8] Unfortunately, Ward only appeared in one game with St. Louis, walking the only batter he faced to open the eighth inning of the July 23, 1935, game against the New York Giants. He returned to the PCL with the Seattle Indians. The following season he arrived in San Diego, where he played for the Padres from 1936 through '39.

The 1937 Padres finished third in the PCL with a 97–81 record, five games behind the first-place Sacramento Solons. In the playoffs, San Diego swept Sacramento in four games, then swept the Portland Beavers to capture the PCL title. Ward, whom *The Sporting News* called "hotter than a house ablaze," fired a four-hitter in the second game of the championship series, striking out five and walking one as San Diego extended its series lead to 2–0.[9]

Heading into the 1938 season, baseball pundits were picking San Diego to repeat as PCL champions unless the San Francisco Seals, who were swept by Portland during the first round in '37, could find additional effective pitching.[10] The 1938 PCL pennant race was close from the start; two weeks into the season the top five clubs were separated by two games, though San Diego and Oakland sank to the basement with 3–12 records, seven games behind Portland.[11] The injury-depleted Padres dramatically improved their position following a nine-game winning streak in late April and early May, which included two 16–1 victories during a May 1 doubleheader against San Francisco as San Diego fielded its full lineup of regulars for the first time all season.[12] The PCL race was hotly contested all season long; on May 9, the Padres held a single-game lead over Los Angeles, Hollywood, and Portland, who were all tied for second place.[13]

BILL SWANK

Dick Ward threw 12⅔ innings of no-hit ball during a 16-inning 1–0 marathon victory over the PCL Los Angeles Angels in 1938.

As August 1938 was winding down, the Los Angeles Angels were enjoying a slight edge over Sacramento for the PCL lead. Following the games played on August 29, the 90–64 Angels maintained a four-game lead over the Solons, with the Padres 10½ games behind Los Angeles.[14] The August 30 series opener between Los Angeles and San Diego marked the beginning of the Angels' final road stretch; they sent southpaw Ray Prim to the mound while initial reports indicated either Jim Chaplin or Howard Craghead would start for the Padres.[15] Prim had struggled with his control during his previous two starts and was eager to improve it against slumping San Diego.

Padres manager Frank Shellenback, who may be best known for his spitball and as Ted Williams's manager, selected Ward to start against the Angels that day. Shellenback had pitched for two seasons with the Chicago White Sox, earning the win against the Cleveland Indians on May 8, 1918, in his major-league debut and pitching in eight games during the 1919 season. He finished 1919 with the Minneapolis Millers in the American Association; as a result, he wasn't listed on a major-league roster when MLB declared the spitball illegal and wasn't among those grandfathered in to continue throwing the pitch legally in the majors.[16] Shellenback pitched in the PCL, where his spitball wasn't banned, through 1938, and managed Hollywood in 1935 and then San Diego in 1936–38 before returning to the majors as a pitching coach. He was a member of the PCL's inaugural Hall of Fame class in 1943, and he holds the record for most career wins (296) and innings pitched (4,184⅓).[17]

Ward started strong, allowing no hits or walks to Los Angeles through four innings. Prim allowed a lone hit during each of the first four frames to San Diego, but the Padres couldn't score. From the fifth through seventh innings, both Ward and Prim kept their opponents hitless. In the ninth inning, the Angels finally had a baserunner when Ward issued his first walk. Prim gave up two hits during the last two innings, but the teams remained scoreless through regulation. Finally, with two outs in the 13th inning, Angels second baseman Eddie Mayo singled to end Ward's no-hit bid. Los Angeles third baseman Charlie English singled in the 14th. The marathon game ended in the 16th inning when Padres right fielder Dom Dallessandro walked, reached second on Joe Berkowitz's sacrifice, reached third on first baseman Spence Harris's bunt, and scored when second baseman Al Niemiec singled him home with the game's only run.[18]

Ward's 12-inning performance remains the longest no-hitter in PCL history.[19] Tough-luck losing pitcher Prim allowed one run on nine hits over 15-plus innings, striking out six and walking five. Ward delivered two base hits, as did Dallessandro and third baseman Joe Berkowitz. Ward also led his team with six assists on the defensive side. Only two of the teams' combined 11 hits went for extra bases: Harris tripled and Dallessandro doubled during regulation. Both teams' leadoff hitters and center fielders, Jigger Statz for Los Angeles and Hal Patchett for San Diego, endured 0-for-7 afternoons.

Ward's gem was not only the longest no-hitter in Padres history, it was also the first. Four more Padres threw no-hitters, although the next one didn't occur until over two decades later. In May 1959, Russ Heman threw a no-hitter against the Vancouver Mounties. Later that month, on the same evening that the Pittsburgh Pirates' Harvey Haddix delivered 12 perfect innings before losing 1–0 to the Milwaukee Braves in 13, Padres pitcher Dick Stigman no-hit Salt Lake through 10⅔ innings, and continued to shut out the Bees through the 12th before Pete Wojey relieved him in the 13th. The Padres eventually defeated the Bees, 1–0, in 15 innings.[20] Table 1 lists the five no-hitters for the PCL Padres.

Interestingly, the definition of a no-hitter varies between the majors and the Pacific Coast League. In

Table 1. PCL San Diego Padres No-Hitters[21]

Date	Pitcher	Opponent	SD Outcome	Starter No-hit Innings	Starter Innings Pitched	Starter Hits Allowed
8/30/1938	Dick Ward	Los Angeles Angels	Won 1–0	12.2	16	2
5/7/1959	Russ Heman	Vancouver Mounties	Won 2–0	9	9	0
5/26/1959	Dick Stigman	Salt Lake City Bees	Won 1–0	10.2	12	1
8/26/1961	Al Worthington	Hawaii Islanders	Won 5–0	9	9	0
8/14/1962	Sammy Ellis	Tacoma Giants	Won 4–0	9	9	0

September 1991 under MLB commissioner Fay Vincent, the MLB committee on statistical accuracy provided the first official definition of a no-hitter, which declared "a no-hitter to be a game of nine innings or more that ends with no hits," which eliminates games that were shortened by rain, darkness, or other reasons; losing efforts by the away team when the home team leads after 8½ innings; and games where a hit was yielded in extra innings.[22] Using MLB's definition, Ward's accomplishment would not be classified as a no-hitter.

The major-league Padres have endured 20 no-hitter close calls, when San Diego pitchers have carried a no-hitter into the eighth inning or beyond, from Kirby's eight no-hit innings in 1970 to Odrisamer Despaigne's 7⅔ innings of no-hit baseball in 2014, also against the Mets, before Daniel Murphy doubled. Padres pitchers have pitched 28 one-hitters since 1969.[23]

Table 2 lists the five Padres no-hit bids that were spoiled in the ninth inning. An odd quirk is that the Padres have never shut out their opponent after losing a no-hit bid in the ninth.

Table 2. MLB San Diego Padres No-Hit Bids Lost During 9th Inning

Date	Pitcher(s)	Opponent	SD Outcome
7/21/1970	Clay Kirby	New York Mets	Lost 3–0
Spoiler	Bud Harrelson singled with 0 outs		
7/18/1972	Steve Arlin	Philadelphia Phillies	Won 5–1
Spoiler	Denny Doyle singled with 2 outs		
9/5/1997	Andy Ashby	Atlanta Braves	Won 6–2
Spoiler	Kenny Lofton signed with 0 outs		
9/22/2006	Chris Young	Pittsburgh Pirates	Won 6–2
Spoiler	Joe Randa homered with 1 out		
7/9/2011	Combined	Los Angeles Dodgers	Lost 1–0
Spoiler	Juan Uribe doubled with 2 outs		

Ward's PCL record 12⅔ no-hit innings broke the record of 10 thrown by the Beavers' Al Carson in 1909 and by the Oakland Oaks' Bill Prough in 1916.[24] Ward pitched one more season in the PCL, starting the year with San Diego before returning to the Angels and finishing his career. He compiled an 80–58 record over 186 games and 1,092 innings covering eight different minor-league seasons. ∎

Additional References

2018 Pacific Coast League Sketch & Record Book.

Baseball Reference: http://www.baseball-reference.com.

Beverage, Richard. *The Los Angeles Angels of the Pacific Coast League: A History, 1903-1957.* Jefferson, NC: McFarland & Company, 2011.

Johnson, Lloyd and Miles Wolff. *Encyclopedia of Minor League Baseball: The Official Record of Minor League Baseball* (Third Edition). Durham, NC: Baseball America, 2007.

Retrosheet: http://www.retrosheet.org/.

SABR Baseball Games Project: http://sabr.org/gamesproject.

San Diego Union-Tribune.

Notes

1. Combined News Services, "Arlin's no-hit bid spoiled by Phils in ninth," *Independent* (Long Beach, CA), July 19, 1972.
2. Tom Saladino, "Gomez Lifts No-Hit Hurler In 8th," *Fresno Bee*, July 22, 1970.
3. Associated Press, "Dick Ward Sets Record," *Oakland Tribune*, August 31, 1938.
4. "Pacific Coast League No-Hit Games," MILB.com, http://www.milb.com/content/page.jsp?ymd=20080317&content_id=361099&sid=l112&vkey=league1.
5. Ralph Huston, "Angel Pitchers and Catchers Report Today," *Los Angeles Times*, February 29, 1932.
6. United Press, "Angels Recall Pitcher," *Santa Maria* (CA) *Times*, August 22, 1932: 6.
7. Associated Press, "Angels Release Four Recruits," *San Francisco Examiner*, April 8, 1932; United Press, "Angels Recall Pitcher," *Santa Maria Times*, August 22, 1932.
8. Dick Farrington, "Davis Slated To Go In Next Card Deal," *The Sporting News*, November 29, 1934.
9. Earl Keller, "Hot Padres Capture Play-off And Title," *The Sporting News*, October 7, 1937.
10. Eddie Murphy, "Oaks Face Solons at Capital In League Opener Tomorrow," *Oakland Tribune*, April 1, 1938.
11. "Standings," *Los Angeles Times*, April 17, 1938.
12. "Padre Win Streak Ends,"*Los Angeles Times*, May 9, 1938; Earl Keller, "Padres Win Column Padded By 9 In Row," *The Sporting News*, May 12, 1938.
13. "Major, Coast League Races," *Los Angeles Times*, May 9, 1938.
14. "Major, Coast League Races," *Oakland Tribune*, August 30, 1938.
15. Bob Ray, "Stars, Suds Mix Tonight," *Los Angeles Times*, August 30, 1938.
16. Brian McKenna, "Frank Shellenback," SABR BioProject, https://sabr.org/bioproj/person/4489ca47.
17. "Frank Shellenback," MILB.com, http://www.milb.com/content/page.jsp?sid=l112&ymd=20110804&content_id=22740344&vkey=league3.
18. Associated Press, "Dick Ward Hurls Padres to 1-0 Victory, 16 Innings," *San Francisco Examiner*, August 31, 1938.
19. Pacific Coast League No-Hit Games, MILB.com.
20. United Press International, "San Diegan Shares Haddix' Feelings," *Herald and News* (Klamath Falls, OR), May 27, 1959.
21. Associated Press, "Dick Ward Sets Record," *Oakland Tribune*, August 31, 1938; Associated Press, "Russ Heman Hurls No-Hit, No-Run Game in PCL," *Arizona Daily Star* (Tucson, AZ), May 8, 1959; UPI, "San Diegan Shares Haddix' Feelings"; "Al Worthington Hurls No-Hitter," *Los Angeles Times*, August 27, 1961; Associated Press, "Padres' Ellis In No-Hitter," *Los Angeles Times*, August 15, 1962.
22. Dick Lammers, "No-Nos Knocked Off the Books," in *No-Hitters*, ed. Bill Nowlin (Phoenix: SABR, 2017), 518–23.
23. "History & Records: Low-Hit Games," in Darren Feeney, ed., *2018 San Diego Padres Media Guide* (San Diego: San Diego Padres, 2018), 210.
24. Associated Press, "San Diego Moundman Chalks Up Record In Whitewashing Angels," *Medford Mail Tribune* (Medford, OR), August 31, 1938.

Bill Starr

The San Diego Padre Who Batted for Ted Williams and Integrated the PCL

Gary Sarnoff

In December 1936, the San Diego Padres of the Pacific Coast League purchased a catcher from the Albany Senators. Bill Starr would leave his mark on San Diego baseball history. As a player, he had the honor of pinch-hitting for Ted Williams. As an owner, he signed the player who broke the Pacific Coast League color barrier.

He was born February 16, 1911, to Russian-Jewish immigrant parents.[1] His given name was Isadore, which he was called until he changed it to William as an adult.[2] His baseball playing records note him as Chick Starr; the sportswriters always referred to him as Bill Starr.

The baseball bug entered Starr's bloodstream while he was growing up on Chicago's West Side. He played the game day and night and became an ardent White Sox fan. One September day in 1920, he was devastated when he heard, "Extra! Extra! Read all about it! White Sox players indicted!" He didn't believe it, but soon the truth was revealed that eight members of the White Sox had conspired to lose the 1919 World Series, and his reaction was "stunned disbelief."[3]

In 1931, Starr signed a contract with Terre Haute of the Three-I League. He reported as a third baseman but was switched to catcher.[4] He spent four and a half years climbing the minor-league ladder before being called up by the Washington Nationals. He played 12 games for the 1935 Nats, and although he was on the Washington roster for almost two months during the first half of the 1936 season, he played in only one game, as a late-inning substitute. He was sent back to Albany for the season's second half, but Albany sent him to Trenton. Starr refused to report and sat out the rest of the season. Thereupon he was sold to San Diego, putting him on a course for destiny.

Starr played three seasons for the Padres, from 1937 to 1939. In a game during the 1937 season, the Padres were batting in the bottom of the ninth inning of a tie game. There was a runner on first, nobody out, and the batter, Ted Williams, had an 0–1 count. Padres manager Frank Shellenback decided this was a bunting situation and Starr was a better candidate for the job. Williams was called to the bench; Starr went to the plate and bunted a foul ball for strike two. Given the swing sign with an 0–2 count, he swung and lifted a fly ball to the outfield for an easy out. Starr failed in his assignment but always enjoyed talking about the moment when he hit for Ted Williams.[5]

That year, a San Diego businessman asked Starr what he was going to do after the season. "I'm going to go home to get married and find a job," Starr said. "Get married, come to San Diego and work for me—I'll make a salesman out of you," replied the businessman. "I was given a job in the credit department," said Starr. "Did that for three years, retired from baseball and started my own collection business."[6]

Starr did very well in that business. "He went door-to-door to collect," said his son, Norman, "and he was very persuasive."[7] Starr's timing was perfect. The Great Depression was over and he benefitted from California's fast-growing economy. Starr, excused from World War II by the draft board due to an injury sustained during the 1938 season, took full advantage of the opportunity and saved enough to bid for ownership of

Bill Starr was a light-hitting catcher throughout his baseball career, however, he did pinch hit for Ted Williams. More significant to Padres history, though, was that after his playing days were over, Starr bought the team.

the Padres. He formed a group of investors, but he needed additional financial backing. "I went to the San Diego Trust and Savings Bank and asked for the bank president, but he didn't know me. I told him I wanted to borrow money to buy a ball club. He looked at me and said, 'I can't loan you money to buy a baseball club, but go down the street to this other bank and ask for Mr. Smith.'"

Starr went down the street, asked for Mr. Smith, and was directed to his office. He sat down, introduced himself and asked for a loan. Without hesitation, C. Arnholt Smith, who would own the Padres one day, beckoned a cashier to his office. "This young man wants to buy a ball club and needs $150,000," Smith told the cashier, "give him a cashier's check."[8] Starr and his group paid $210,000 for the Padres.[9]

One year later, Starr took notice when Branch Rickey signed Jackie Robinson to the Brooklyn Dodgers. "What would happen if I searched out and found some capable black players?" Starr wondered. "The coast was very lily-white and some of the old-timers were very critical of Rickey," Starr would later say. "I thought it was kind of stupid."[10]

The Padres' owner had the perfect player in mind: Johnny Ritchey, a clean-cut catcher and San Diego native who starred at San Diego high school and San Diego State. "He has fair speed, can hit, has a good arm and he hustles," one sportswriter offered.[11] He was also said to be talented, enthusiastic, and always smiling. In 1947, Ritchey was leading the Negro American League in batting average. Starr sent scouts to look him over, and after the reports came back, he signed Ritchey for the 1948 season. "We believe we signed one of the finest prospects in the country," said Starr. "His record at San Diego High School, San Diego State and the Chicago Negro League team has been particularly outstanding."

Starr made it clear that he was not doing this to be a crusader: "We are not sponsoring any causes. Our interest in Ritchey is primarily that he can swing that bat."[12] Starr was happy to learn that all six hotels the Padres occupied on the road would welcome Ritchey. "If he's good enough to play for your team, he is more than welcome at our hotel," said a San Francisco hotel manager.

Things went well for the rookie catcher during spring training. "He is definitely one of the gang," said Padres manager, Ripper Collins. "Everyone has been swell to me," said Ritchey. "I can't ask for better treatment. In exhibition games, most of the customers were on my side, and the umpires offered me all kinds of encouragement. All the players have cooperated with

Johnny Ritchey, a catcher for the 1948 and 1949 Padres, broke the Pacific Coast color barrier. Starr had been impressed by Branch Rickey's signing of Jackie Robinson and wanted to follow suit.

me. I did expect a little friction, but I haven't encountered it yet."[13] The sportswriters were also for him. "It's one of the many signs that America is coming of age, and the promise that other and even more formidable walls will come tumbling down," wrote Nat Low of the *Daily Worker*. Asked if Ritchey would be the Padres' starting catcher, Collins wouldn't comment. "Johnny can hit, anyone can see that, and he's strong," said Collins. "But he's young and I haven't seen him in a game yet."[14] Ritchey wasn't the team's number one catcher, even after he started the season by going 5-for-8. "If he keeps up this good hitting, he'll be the team's number one catcher," the *San Diego Evening Tribune* noted.[15]

The good treatment of spring training disappeared when the season began. Ritchey was spiked and constantly harassed. Pitchers threw at him. He was standing on second after hitting a double when an opposing pitcher walked over and unloaded with bad language. The biggest culprit was Los Angeles shortstop Bill Schuster, "a terrible person," according to Ritchey.[16] Most bothersome to Ritchey was the lack of support from his teammates, who never said a thing or retaliated on his behalf. It also troubled him that he roomed alone and his teammates hardly spoke to him. In addition, he was unhappy being an every-other-day player. "I sensed a coolness, a distancing that was apparent to him," a teammate said. "He smiled less and didn't seem to have much fun."[17] On the bright side, he was popular with the fans, especially with children, who often mobbed him for an autograph.[18]

Before the 1949 season, Starr wanted his club to become affiliated with a major-league team. He considered the Cleveland Indians a perfect fit. The Padres were the first team to break the PCL color barrier, the Indians the first to do so in the American League. Cleveland, with 14 black players under contract, was hunting for a new triple-A affiliate, one that Indians brass knew would take care of their prospects.[19] Starr knew Indians owner Bill Veeck from the days when Veeck owned the minor-league Milwaukee Brewers. He was also friendly with Indians general manager Hank Greenberg, but there was an obstacle: Greenberg was a close friend of Hollywood Stars owner Bob Cobb, who also pitched the Indians for affiliation. Using his negotiating and sales experience, Starr managed to seal the deal. "We selected San Diego because we felt that Bill Starr would be most interested in seeing that our players would be properly developed and it seems to have the most to offer," said Greenberg.[20] He added, "Bill Starr was extremely anxious to have the Padres join the Cleveland organization."[21] To put the final touch on the deal, Bucky Harris, who had won the 1924 World Series as a player-manager with the Nationals and the 1947 Series as the manager of the New York Yankees, agreed to manage the Padres. "We feel San Diego has the best set-up in minor-league baseball," said Starr. "First arranging a working agreement with the world champion Cleveland Indians and getting a world champion manager in Bucky Harris."[22]

The Padres had 34 players on their roster, and now the Indians would assign players to San Diego, meaning there would not be spots for everyone. Ritchey, however, was projected as a mainstay.[23] He was the only Padre to receive a pay raise in 1949.[24] When spring training began, the catcher made a huge impression. "Ritchey is better than any catcher we had on the Yankees last season," Harris said.[25] He also predicted that Ritchey would be the Indians' starting catcher by 1951.[26]

In addition to Ritchey, the 1949 Padres had three other black ballplayers. The Indians sent first baseman Luke Easter, smooth-fielding shortstop Artie Wilson, and outfielder Minnie Miñoso. Easter was 6-foot-4, 240 pounds, and could hit the ball a country mile. Before the season, Starr warned Easter about harassment he might endure over the color of his skin. "Mr. Starr," said Easter, "everyone likes me when I hit the ball."[27] Easter was right. His power made him a huge drawing card around the circuit. In Los Angeles, a record crowd of 23,083 clicked the turnstiles to see him hit.[28] "We opened the ballpark early so people could watch Easter hit" during batting practice, said Starr. To add to the show, Starr came up with the idea of having Easter hit special baseballs, called Goldsmith balls. "It was a much livelier ball, almost like a golf ball," Starr

said. "When it was Easter's turn to hit, our coach, Red Corriden, would give the pitcher the Goldsmith balls. Luke would drive that ball out of sight and the people in the stands would go oooh and ahhhh! But we had to stop that because pretty soon the other hitters started saying that they wanted the Goldsmith balls."[29] Easter played only 80 games before the Indians called him up.

Miñoso was sent down for seasoning after starting the season in Cleveland.[30] "I appreciated San Diego because it opened a new door for me," he said. "People in San Diego were so nice. Bill Starr was a good man."

Starr was concerned that the 23-year-old Miñoso would be influenced by the fast-living Easter, who was well into his 30s. "You're a nice fellow," Starr told Miñoso shortly after he arrived. "I don't want you hanging around Easter. I don't want you getting his bad habits." Miñoso ignored the advice and stayed out with Easter one night. The next day he went 1-for-5; Easter went 4-for-5. Realizing that Starr was right, he stayed away from Easter and his nightlife. Johnny Ritchey, on the other hand, was a guy he liked to be around. "He was a nice guy," Miñoso said. "He had blue eyes [actually, green]. He was quiet and was a good left-handed hitting catcher." He also liked his manager. "Harris was a clean and decent guy who looked like he came from Hollywood," Miñoso said. One day in Oakland, with two on and a 3–0 count, Miñoso was given the take sign but swung away and made a hit that scored both runners. "Nice going," Harris told Miñoso, "but in the big leagues you'll be fined $500."[31]

In 1949, Ritchey was once again a part-time player. The following season he was sent to Portland, where again he spent the season as a part-timer. He found happiness in 1951 when he was sent to Vancouver of the Western International League. Although it was a lower-tier minor league, it gave Ritchey the chance to play every day. A strange circumstance developed when Bill Schuster, the former Angels shortstop who'd been Ritchey's biggest PCL antagonist, was hired to manage the team. By that time, Schuster had learned the error of his ways, and the two men got along, "But my dad never forgot the way Schuster treated him" in the Pacific Coast League, said Johanna Ritchey Battle.[32]

Following the 1951 season, the Indians elected to relocate their triple-A affiliation to Indianapolis. They thanked San Diego for its support and said they enjoyed working with Bill Starr, but claimed the traveling distance was too great a burden. The Padres were once again an independent PCL team.[33]

The Padres continued to employ black baseball players. "Regardless of race or color, I'll give any promising player a chance to make the grade," Starr said.[34]

In 1952, he paid $100 to a lower-tier minor-league team for first baseman Tom Alston. Two years later, Alston became the first African American to play for the Cardinals when he was traded to St. Louis for two other players and $100,000, plus two players on optional assignment. At the time, it was the biggest deal ever made for a minor-league player.[35]

In 1954, Luke Easter returned to San Diego. "I am very happy to be coming back," he said. And he started where he had left off. After stepping off a train at 7:05 AM, he played in the game that afternoon and hit a 490-foot home run.[36] He continued to thrill the fans with his moon shots, including the longest home run hit at San Diego's Lane Field. "He hit it out of the park," said Phil Starr, one of Bill's three sons, who watched it from the press box. "It cleared a highway, a set of tracks and hit a freight shed. It was the furthest home run I ever saw."[37]

In the mid-1950s, Starr began to lobby for a new ballpark. He claimed Lane Field was outdated and infested with termites. His vision was a new facility in Balboa Park. He was turned down twice by the city but did not give up. "If I fail to get a new ballpark, I'll sell," he said. When he was turned down a third time, he told a friend, "I'm beginning to lose interest." He appeared less often at Lane Field and did not attend the 1955 PCL midseason meeting. In August 1955, Starr sold the Padres to Westgate California Tuna Packing Company for $250,000. The press noted that it was not a desperation sale. The Padres had money in the bank and would show a profit in 1955. Starr was rumored to be the next PCL president, but he said he wanted no part of it. "I don't know what I will do," he told sportswriters. "Know where I can get a job starting September 12th?" he said with a smile.[38]

After baseball, Starr became one of the first condominium builders in the country. He also built shopping centers and became a wealthy man. He was active in the Jewish community and was one of the founders and president of the San Diego Jewish Community Center. He was a board member of both the San Diego Chamber of Commerce and the Convention and Business Bureau. Bill Starr died in 1991 at the age of 80. ∎

Notes

1. Erwin Lynn, *Jewish Baseball Hall of Fame* (New York: Shapolsky Publishers, 1987), 66.
2. Medill High School Yearbook, *Medillite* (Chicago, 1928).
3. Bill Starr, *Clearing the Bases* (New York: Michael Kesend Publishing, 1989), 1.
4. *San Diego Evening Tribune*, September 26, 1944.
5. Starr, 8.
6. Jim Smith and Bill Ohler, "Bill Starr" (1990 interview), San Diego History Center, 1995. http://www.sandiegohistory.org/journal/1995/january/starr-2/.
7. Norman Starr, telephone interview with the author, April 27, 2009.
8. Ray Brandes and Bill Swank, *The Pacific Coast League San Diego Padres Volume I* (San Diego: San Diego Historical Society, 1996), 30.
9. "Control of Padres Sold to Tuna Cannier; O'Doul May Take Charge," *Los Angeles Times*, August 25, 1955.
10. Bill Swank, *Echoes From Lane Field* (Paducah, Kentucky: Turner, 1999).
11. Nat Low, "The Low Down," *Daily Worker*, March 9, 1947.
12. Leon Washington Jr., "Johnny Ritchey interviewed by Sentinel editor," *Los Angeles Sentinel*, date unknown, National Baseball Hall of Fame and Library, Giamae Research Center, Cooperstown, New York.
13. Charley Gregg, *Straight From the Shoulder*, date and publication unknown, Giamae Research Center.
14. Low, "The Low Down."
15. *San Diego Evening Tribune*, April 3, 1948.
16. Swank, *Echoes From Lane Field*.
17. Ray Brandes and Bill Swank, *The Pacific Coast League San Diego Padres Volume II* (San Diego: San Diego Historical Society, 1997), 39.
18. Gregg, *Straight From the Shoulder*.
19. Rick Swaine, *The Integralon of Major League Baseball* (Jefferson, North Carolina: McFarland, 2009).
20. *San Diego Union*, November 17, 1948.
21. "Padres Ballclub Arrange Pact With Indians," *Los Angeles Times*, November 17, 1948.
22. Al Wolf, "Bucky Harris is greeted by bushels of praise," *Los Angeles Times*, February 8, 1949.
23. *San Diego Union*, November 17, 1948.
24. Brandes and Swank, *Volume II*, 82.
25. Brandes and Swank, *Volume II*, 90.
26. *Hits hard in clutch during first stretch*, publication and date unknown, National Baseball Hall of Fame and Library, Giamae Research Center.
27. Dominic Cotton, "So, maybe there really is such a thing as 'the Natural'?" *Smithsonian*, July 2011.
28. Brandes and Swank, *Volume II*, 91.
29. Brandes and Swank, *Volume II*, 85.
30. Mark Stewart, "Minnie Minoso," SABR BioProject, https://sabr.org/bioproj/person/796bd066
31. Brandes and Swank, *Volume II*, 109–11.
32. Johannaa Ritchey Battle, interview with the author, San Diego, May 17, 2017.
33. Brandes and Swank, *Volume II*, 170.
34. Earl Keller, "Ritchey Became the First Negro to Sign Coast League Pact," *San Diego Evening Tribune*, date unknown.
35. Brandes and Swank, *Volume II*, 264.
36. Brandes and Swank, *Volume II*, 283.
37. Phil Starr, telephone interview with the author, May 13, 2009.
38. *San Diego Evening Tribune*, August 25, 1955.

The San Diego Tigers of the West Coast Negro Baseball League

Leslie Heaphy

As World War II ended, baseball was moving in a new direction. The Brooklyn Dodgers' signing of Jackie Robinson launched a new era of integration for the National Pastime, the first step in a long journey that is still in progress. Since the doors to the majors would not open right away, there continued to be a need for opportunities for non-white players. Abe Saperstein, owner of the Harlem Globetrotters, began to work with local businessmen in California in late 1945 to create a West Coast League, which would begin play in 1946 as a way to continue to offer chances for African American ballplayers.

Though the plan for the league was for a full season and beyond, only half of one season would be played, from May to July 1946, with six teams participating. Due to its short tenure, little has been written about the league and not a great deal of sources exist to explain its importance in the history of baseball.

Black baseball in California has a history that dates to the nineteenth century. Much of the play centered on San Francisco and Los Angeles during the winter. The California (later Pacific Coast) Winter League was the place for organized games. African American teams regularly played in the league, with Rube Foster bringing his Leland Giants out to play in 1910. The Chicago American Giants came out in 1912–13 to play 24 games against the San Diego Bears, the 1911 winners of the California Winter League. The Giants left San Diego with a 14–10 record. Walter Johnson found himself on the losing end of the score against the Los Angeles Giants during the 1908–09 winter season. This foundation of integrated play helped spur the creation of the West Coast League in 1946. There were also a number of smaller semipro leagues that played all over California, such as the Berkeley International Colored League.[1]

Local businessmen and sports promoters in California began meeting in October 1945 to discuss creating a league for African American ballplayers. They used the first meetings to discern interest and begin to discuss key details, such as where the teams would play, who would be in charge and so on. The official creation took place at the High Marine Social Club in Oakland in early 1946. Led by two Berkeley firemen, Eddie Harris and David Portlock, a league structure was created. The original plan included a 110-game schedule with all member teams paying a $500 franchise fee. The official name of the league was the West Coast Baseball Association. There were some big names involved—Saperstein, Jesse Owens, Negro Leaguers such as Hal "Yellowhorse" Morris and local star Herb Simpson—and the organizing group thought they would help drive interest.

The schedule was not completed and the franchise fee was not regularly collected. One argument for the failure of the league would be the rush to put it together in just a couple of months. The original group did vote to make Saperstein president, Owens vice president, and Portlock league secretary, but details such as securing stadiums and umpires for the games and creating publicity for the league were not ironed out ahead of time, leaving teams scrambling during the season to stay on top of all that was needed. Telegrams between Saperstein and Oakland Larks business manager Ed Harris make the lack of business planning clear. They talk about games being canceled, stadiums being unavailable, and salary disputes involving players asking for more money than the league could pay.[2]

The six original teams represented Seattle, Portland, Oakland, San Francisco, Fresno, and Los Angeles. The San Diego Tigers took over for the Fresno team before the season even began, under the leadership of Roy Parker. The San Diego club played a doubleheader against the Oakland Larks in the season opener on May 12, 1946, at Fresno Midget Auto Racing Park. The Tigers won the first game, 8–7, and lost the second, 3–0. The crowd was estimated at 2,500 fans.[3] A third game may have been lost by a score of 21–4. Results for other games have not been found as coverage of the league was sporadic and centered mainly around the more well-known Oakland Larks. For example, we know Owens's Portland Rosebuds started their season with three games in El Paso, Texas. Their league schedule had them playing the Seattle Steelheads. By the time the league folded, the Larks were promoting themselves as the winners of the league with a reported 14–3 record. The Tigers were listed in fifth place at 4–6, ahead of only the Los Angeles White Sox, who finished 3–12.[4]

When the West Coast league folded, some of the teams, including the Tigers, continued to play barnstorming schedules. Ads appeared in several California papers in September 1946 announcing the Tigers playing in San Bernardino, Salinas, and Santa Maria. One of the games in Salinas had to be halted: Umpire Ace Johnson stopped it because of the name-calling from the stands. Salinas fans cheered the Tigers players after the game and apologized for the behavior of people they felt were clearly not from Salinas. Salinas did end up winning the game, 7–5, on a two-run homer by Doc Tucker in the seventh inning.[5]

The team returned to play in 1947 as well. One of the highlights the team used in advertising was the great play of one-armed fielder Jesse Alexander, who before the game and between innings would show off his fielding and powerful hitting.[6] In early July, the Tigers found themselves returning from a tour of Southern states and Mexico, where the local papers reported they had won 80 percent of the games they played. A newspaper in Oregon reported big crowds were expected when the Tigers came to town because of the great success they'd had on their tour.[7]

The San Diego Tigers had a short existence but played a key role in the growth of black baseball on the West Coast. The team enjoyed a measure of success that gave fans a chance to see some of their local players realize their dreams of playing professional baseball. Much more study needs to be done to learn about this team and its players to add to the history of black baseball. ∎

Notes

1. "Looking Back: California's Negro League," San Jose Public Library. https://www.sjpl.org/blog/lookingback-californias-negro-league; "African American Baseball in San Diego," San Diego History Center; By-laws, Correspondence 1945–1947, West Coast Negro Baseball Association Collection, MS 17, African American Museum & Library at Oakland, Oakland Public Library, Oakland, California. https://oac.cdlib.org/findaid/ark:/13030/c8125j5/.
2. Guide to the West Coast Negro Baseball Association Collection, West Coast Negro Baseball Association Collection.
3. Guide.
4. Undated press releases, West Coast Negro Baseball Association collection; Won-Loss Record, Center for Negro League Research, Birmingham, Alabama; Milan Simonich, "EP was Home to the Negro Leagues for One Weekend," El Paso Times, July 12, 2010. https://www.elpasotimes.com/story/news/history/blogs/tales-from-themorgue/2013/06/24/ep-was-home-to-the-negro-leagues-for-one-weekend/31495787/.
5. "Salinas Rallys in Seventh to Turn Back Tigers, 7–5," Salinas Californian, September 3, 1946.
6. "Handicap no Hex," Santa Maria Daily Times and Courier, May 10, 1947
7. "San Diego Tigers Battle Umpqua Chiefs," Roseburg News Review, July 5, 1947.
8. Compiled from a variety of newspaper sources as no official rosters have been found.

San Diego Tigers Roster[8]

Name	Position	Year
Alexander, Jesse	INF/OF	1946–47
Brown, J.		1946
Curtis, Harvey	CF	1947
Flowers, W.	3B	1947
Floyd, Albert	1B	1947
Gabe, Ted		1946
Gray, Chappie	SS	1947
Green, Bill	P/LF	1946
Gross, Roy		1946
Hayden, Pop	P	1947
Hernandez, Benny		1946
Hicks, Wilbur		1946
Lawson, ?	P	1948
Litspey, John	P	1947
Lowe, Jack	C	1946–47
Malone, Lucky	P/1B	1946–47
McDonald, ?	RF	1946
Mouton, Anthony	P	1946
Mouton, Stanley		1946
Pierce, ?	P	1948
Poole, Milton	OF/P	1946–47
Taylor, Kenny	P	1947
Thomas, M. L.	RF	1947
Walker, ?	3B	1946
Wallace, ?	C	1948
Walton, George	2B/P	1946–47
Watkins, Ed	RF	1946

San Diego Breaks Pacific Coast League Color Barrier

Alan Cohen

On March 30, 2005, the Padres unveiled a bust of Johnny Ritchey at the recently opened Petco Park, two years after his death. On February 21, 2017, Ritchey was inducted into the Breitbard Hall of Fame in San Diego. Why was Ritchie memorialized so? He was the Pacific Coast League's barrier breaker in terms of color.

The year after Jackie Robinson broke the major-league color barrier in 1947, the Cleveland Indians bought Minnie Miñoso from the New York Cubans of the Negro National League. Miñoso, who had been an infielder with the Cubans, would be moved to the outfield when he joined the Indians at the beginning of the 1949 season. Miñoso needed tutelage, which he received in San Diego after joining the Indians' Triple-A affiliate in mid-May 1949. He and Luke Easter formed the nucleus of the Padres—who would advance to the Pacific Coast League playoffs for the first time since 1942—but they were not the first black players with the Padres. On November 22, 1947, the Padres had signed San Diego's Ritchey to a contract. Ritchey, a catcher, played in 103 games in 1948, batting .323. He spent parts of seven seasons in the Pacific Coast League but never got the call to play in the majors.

As a youngster in San Diego, Ritchey—who was born on January 5, 1923—had starred in American Legion ball and was on teams that advanced far in tournaments in 1938 and 1940. In 1940, he was barred because of his color from participating in the championship game. As Wendell Smith noted in the *Pittsburgh Courier*, "The American Legion bowed to un-Americanism again last week by permitting the Legion of Albermarle, N.C., to bar San Diego's two colored stars, Johnny Ritchey and Nelson Manuel. Playing down in Albermarle, N.C., the two colored kids were benched because the Southerners didn't want to play against them. The San Diego Legion submitted to Albermarle's demands."[1]

After graduating from high school in 1941, Ritchey went to San Diego State College, but his college career was interrupted after one year by service in the army during World War II. After the war, he returned to school and led his team in batting with a .356 average in 1946. He left San Diego State in 1947 and signed on with the Chicago American Giants of the Negro American League, with whom he had a great season. When his team completed the final game of the home season on September 14, Ritchey was sporting a .376 batting average, best in the Negro American League.[2]

Interest in his talents was shown by the Chicago Cubs, with whom he tried out September 19, but he elected to sign with Bill Starr, president of the Pacific Coast League's San Diego Padres. At the time of the signing, Starr said, "We believe we have signed one of the finest prospects in the country. We are not sponsoring any causes. Our interest in Ritchey is primarily that he can swing that bat. He is a potential major league prospect and has a better than reasonable chance of helping the Padres."[3]

It was anticipated that he would be sent down to the Padres' Tacoma affiliate in the Western International League, but Ritchey stayed with San Diego. He officially broke the league's color line when, appearing as a pinch-hitter on March 30, 1948, he grounded out in the first game of the PCL season.[4] Then, due to injuries to catchers Len Rice in the first game and Hank Camelli in the second game, only Earl Kuper and Ritchey were available to catch. Kuper replaced Camelli in the second game, a 17–2 loss, and Ritchey got his first hit as a pinch-hitter in the same game. Ritchey's first start was the following day. He tripled and singled in a 12–5 win. He went on a hitting spree and his numbers for the first five games of the season were remarkable. He went 7-for-11 with a double, a triple, and a homer. Although he was relegated to the bench when Rice and Camelli returned to action, Ritchey appeared in 103 of his team's 188 games, and his .323 batting average was second best on the team. On Opening Day in 1949, the Padres had three black faces in the starting lineup. Johnny Ritchey was back for his second season with the team and he was joined by Luke Easter and Artie Wilson.

In 1949, when the Padres formalized their affiliation with Bill Veeck's Cleveland Indians, they demolished the color line. The pipeline established, Veeck and his general manager, Hank Greenberg, would funnel player after player to San Diego for years. Some were destined for major-league stardom. Others would have a cup of coffee in the big leagues. Still others, often past their prime when they played with the Padres, would not get to the big leagues.

Luscious Easter, at age 33, came to the team after having played with the Homestead Grays of the Negro National League for two years. Prior to 1947, he had been somewhat under the radar, having a nomadic experience in Negro baseball dating back to 1937, when he began playing for a St. Louis team that spent much time barnstorming. In 1946, he had played with the independent Cincinnati Crescents. In 1948, when the Homestead Grays won the last Negro League World Series, Easter played in both East-West All-Star games.

He didn't last the whole season with the Padres. In early August, he was called up to the big leagues by the Indians after batting .363 with 25 homers and 92 RBIs in 80 games for San Diego. From 1950 through 1952, he slugged 86 homers and drove in 307 runs. In 1954, at age 38 he was sent back to San Diego by the Indians and banged out 13 homers in 56 games. His career was not over, not by a long shot. At age 40, he became the scourge of the International League,

NATIONAL BASEBALL HALL OF FAME AND LIBRARY, COOPERSTOWN, NY

Luke Easter at bat for the Indians.

slugging 35 or more homers in three successive seasons with Buffalo. He struck his last homers with Rochester at age 47 in 1963 and retired after the 1964 season.

Early in 1949, Veeck had signed infielder Artie Wilson, who had been a headliner in the Negro Leagues, finishing second in the league in batting in 1945 with a .372 average as reported by the *Pittsburgh Courier*.[5] Veeck also signed Easter around the same time, but little notice was paid to Luke until he batted .474 in March as the Padres prepped for the season.

Wilson was not with the Padres for long. The Yankees had disputed his signing by Veeck and gained rights to the shortstop. The Yankees sold Wilson to Oakland of the Pacific Coast League, where he became the first player of color with the Oaks, batting .350. His overall average for 1949, .348, put him atop the league's batters. Wilson did not enjoy success in the majors. He played briefly for the New York Giants. His first game was on April 18, 1951. After playing in his 19th game on May 23, he was sent back to the minors when Willie Mays was called up to the Giants. Wilson also broke the color line with Seattle, for whom he played from 1952 through 1954, and with Portland in 1955.

After the 1949 season was under way, the Padres added Miñoso to the lineup. He made it to the majors to stay in 1951, but after less than a month with the Indians, he was traded to the White Sox, with whom he spent most of his career. He was a nine-time American League All-Star, and in 10 of his first 11 full seasons in the majors, he led the league in being hit by pitches. In his first three full seasons, he led the league in stolen bases, and he was the triples leader three times. He could also hit the ball over the fence. He had 186 homers in the majors and had 20 or more in four seasons. When they got around to giving awards for defensive skills, he won three Gold Gloves.

After the 1949 season, Ritchey was traded to the Portland Beavers. Although often said to have major-league talent with the bat, his fielding was suspect, and he tended to throw the ball wildly. He never got the call to the big leagues.

On the mound in 1950 for the Padres was 36-year-old Roy Welmaker, who had been part of the great Homestead Grays teams from 1936 through 1945 and had played in the East-West All-Star game in 1945, pitching two shutout innings. He signed with Cleveland prior to the 1949 season and went 22–12 at Wilkes-Barre in the Class A Eastern League. In 1950 with San Diego, he was 16–10. Although he pitched in the PCL for three more seasons, Welmaker was well past his prime and didn't make it to the majors.

The 1950 Padres finished four games behind the Oaks and had three black outfielders in the vanguard. Miñoso, in his second year with the club, batted .339, fifth in the league, with 20 homers and 115 RBIs in 169 games.

The Indians had plucked Harry Simpson off the roster of the Cubans and he spent 1949 at Wilkes-Barre, leading the league in homers with 31. In 1950 with the Padres, Simpson put up even bigger power numbers than Miñoso, with 33 homers and 156 RBIs in 178 games. The next season, Simpson, who played for five big-league teams over an eight-year span, earning the nickname "Suitcase," was with the Indians.

Completing the trio of great black outfielders on the 1950 Padres was Al Smith, who had played with the Cleveland Buckeyes in the Negro American League and was part of their Negro League World Series championship team in 1947. He was signed by the Indians on July 11, 1948, and spent the balance of that season and 1949 with Wilkes-Barre. After spending 1950 and '51 with the Padres, he was sent to the new top Indians farm team, Indianapolis, in 1952. Midway through 1953, he joined Cleveland.

The connection with the Indians would send more players of color to the Padres in 1951. Sam Jones, who had spent the 1948 season with the Buckeyes, was signed by the Indians and spent the 1950 season with Wilkes-Barre. In 1951, he was with the Padres, going 16–13 with a league-leading 246 strikeouts. Jones had success at the major-league level. After brief trials with the Indians in 1951 and '52, he moved on to the Cubs organization and was named to the National League All-Star team in 1955. In 1959 with the San Francisco Giants, he won 21 games and led the National League in shutouts (4) and ERA (2.83).

Pitcher Henry Miller was with the Padres for a short time in 1951. He was a noted Negro League player, but he only had a brief taste of Organized Baseball. Miller was 33 years old in 1951 and had spent 11 years with the Philadelphia Stars of the Negro National League. He only appeared in six games with the Padres.

Toward the end of the 1951 season, Jose Santiago joined the Padres. He had pitched for the New York Cubans as a teenager in 1947 and '48 and joined the Indians organization prior to the 1949 season. After stops at Dayton and Wilkes-Barre, he joined the Padres, going an unspectacular 1–5. A baseball nomad, he had three trips to the big leagues playing with the Indians for parts of 1954 and '55 and the Athletics for part of 1956.

Negro League superstar Artie Wilson played briefly with San Diego in 1949 and was the first black player for Oakland, Seattle, and Portland.

The Indians temporarily suspended their affiliation with the Padres after 1951, but players of color would continue to be part of the team in the following years.

Theolic Smith came on board in 1952. When he started pitching professionally in 1936, he was part of the Pittsburgh Crawfords. the top team in the middle years of the Negro National League. He appeared in three Negro East-West games and hurled in the Mexican League before coming to the Padres at age 39.

Milt Smith and Tom Alston were also on the 1952 team. They were the first Padres of color without Negro League credentials.

Alston was in his second year of professional ball and joined the Padres midway through the season. He also spent the entire 1953 season with the Padres, batting .297 in 180 games. He played parts of four seasons with the St. Louis Cardinals after becoming, on April 13, 1954, the first player of color to play for the Cardinals.

Milt Smith joined the Padres late in 1952, coming to San Diego from Lewiston, Idaho, in the Western International League, where he had batted .318. In 1953, he once again began the season at a lower level, but once promoted to the Padres, he batted .271 in 55 games. He stayed with the Padres through 1955 and was batting .338 when the Cincinnati Reds brought him up to the majors. He played in 36 games for the Reds in 1955 and was the 61st player to cross the twentieth-century major-league color line.

By this point, the PCL's growing pains in terms of integration were over, and in 1952, three of the league's top four batting averages were posted by persons of color. None of the three was with the Padres, but it was San Diego that had carved the path. In 1954, the Padres tied for first place with the Holly-wood Stars with a 101–67 records, and they defeated the Stars, 7–2, to gain the number one seed in the postseason playoffs. Although they lost in the playoffs to eventual league champion Oakland, they had had an exemplary season led by Luke Easter, Milt Smith, and Theolic Smith.

There was one other player, just coming into pro ball, who was briefly with the Padres in 1954. Floyd Robinson graduated from San Diego High School and signed with the Padres that year. They were unaffili-ated at the time. He spent his first two seasons in the low minors before being called up for short stints at the end of each of those years.

The Indians reestablished their connection with the Padres in 1956 and the affiliation lasted through 1959. In 1956 and '57, Floyd Robinson, now property of the Indians, spent the entire season with the Padres, batting .271 in 1956 and .279 in 1957. It would be a while before Robinson made it to the big leagues. He spent 1958 and '59 in the Marines, and by the time he was released, San Diego was affiliated with the White Sox. Robinson became the property of Chicago. In 1960, Robinson batted .318 and was called up to the Sox at the end of the season. He played nine years in the majors, batting .283, and in 1962 he led the American League in doubles with 45 and was fourth in the league with 109 RBIs.

From 1956 through 1959, more players of color joined the Padres, some on their way down and one on the way up. Dave Hoskins, a pitcher who had begun his career with the Homestead Grays, was with the Indians in 1953 and 1954. In 1956, he was sent to the Padres, for whom he went 7–11.

> In the future, if our Negro players are (not) ac-cepted, there will be no game. These youngsters are just as much a part of our organization as any of the others in camp.[6]
> — Hank Greenberg, April 1953

Billy Harrell was a star in both baseball and bas-ketball at Siena College in New York and was signed by Greenberg after he graduated. In his second minor-league season, spring training in segregated Florida was stressful. Greenberg was supportive of his black players, and when accommodations were denied to Harrell and Brooks Lawrence, Greenberg expressed his indignation. Harrell made it to the Indians in 1955 and

Al Smith played with the Padres 1950-51 and went on to 12-year career in the American League, during which he played in two World Series.

played at San Diego in 1957 before returning to the Indians at the end of that season. He was with the Indians through the end of 1958, after which he re-turned to the minors, having one last bite of the apple with the Red Sox in 1961.

Joe Caffie had some great seasons in the minors, but he only played 44 games in the majors in 1956–57. In 1956, after spending spring training with the Indi-ans, he was farmed out to San Diego. He spent only 19 games with the Padres before being moved to Buffalo in the International League on May 12. He was batting .311 through 128 games with the Bisons when he was called up by Cleveland in September. He batted .342 in 12 games with the Tribe. The following year, after another good season with Buffalo, he appeared in 32 games with the Indians, batting .270.

Dave Pope's career began with the Homestead Grays in 1946 and he first made it to the big leagues with the Indians in 1952. In parts of four seasons, he batted .265 in 230 games, and he played in the 1954 World Series. The Indians sent him to San Diego for the 1957 and '58 seasons and he batted .313 and .316. Unfortunately, he would not return to the big leagues.

Larry Raines was with the Indians in 1957, getting into 96 games, but at the beginning of 1958, he was sent to San Diego, where he batted .303. He got called up to the Indians in September, but only got into seven games. They were his last games in the majors.

On his way up to the big leagues was Jim "Mudcat" Grant. He signed in 1954 and made it to San Diego for the 1957 season. With the Padres, he was 18–7 with a 2.32 ERA. The next year he made his debut with the Indians and was 145–119 in 14 major-league seasons.

In 1957, each PCL team had at least one player of color, following the lead of the San Diego Padres. As

1957 ended, change was on the horizon for the PCL. With the western migration of the major leagues, teams in San Francisco, Los Angeles, and Hollywood would be replaced. San Diego remained in the league through 1968, secure in its legacy of having created opportunities for players of color in the Pacific Coast League. ■

Sources

In additional to Baseball-Reference.com and the sources shown in the notes, the author used:

Costello, Rory. "Sam Jones." SABR Bio-Project.

Engelhardt, Brian. "Billy Harrell," SABR Bio-Project.

Jackson, Josh. "The Year After Jackie, Ritchey Integrated PCL," MiLB.com, February 21, 2018.

Keller, Earl. "Ritchey, Padre Negro, Wrapping Up Regular Mask Job with Steady Raps," *The Sporting News*, April 14, 1948.

Notes

1. Wendell Smith, "Smitty's Sports Spurts," *Pittsburgh Courier*, September 21, 1940.
2. Herman Hill, "John Ritchey: Young Man with a Future; Hits Hard in Clutch During First season," *Pittsburgh Courier*, March 19, 1949.
3. Mitch Angus, "Padres Sign PCL's First Negro Player," *San Diego Union*, November 23, 1947.
4. John B. Old, "Coast Opens to 41,374; Oaks Draw Top Crowd," *The Sporttng News*, April 7, 1948.
5. "Jethroe Retains A. L. Batting Crown; .393 Mark Tops Loop," *Pittsburgh Courier*, September 15, 1945: 12. Statistical records were haphazardly kept in the Negro Leagues. Seamheads.com's Negro Leagues database has Wilson as 10th in batting average for the season with .315.
6. "Greenberg Backs Negro Farm Aces," *Pittsburgh Courier*, April 11, 1953.

Baseball Burials in San Diego

Fred Worth

I hang out in cemeteries. Well, that's not exactly accurate. I go to cemeteries. A lot of them. As of February 15, 2019, I have gone to more than 2,750 cemeteries in 41 states and the District of Columbia in order to find more than 6,200 baseball-related graves. Since the cemeteries are not all along interstates, I get to see a lot of fascinating and beautiful places. It also allows me to connect with baseball history in an unusual way.

In December 2014, I took my first trip to California for grave hunting. Since it was a winter trip, I limited myself to the southern portion of the state, going from San Diego up to the Los Angeles metropolitan area. Since this issue of *The National Pastime* is focusing on San Diego, I will do the same and look at the graves I visited in what many call "America's Finest City."

I have visited 50 "final resting places" in San Diego. They're in seven cemeteries and on one beach, where some of Lou Marone's ashes were scattered. There's a detailed list at the end of this article. Right now I want to look at the graves of 14 of the better-known San Diego burials.

JOE QUEST, MOUNT HOPE CEMETERY

Joe Quest was not a great ballplayer. He played in the National Association in 1871. He then had two stints in the National League and two in the American Association from 1878 through 1886. His .217 lifetime batting average does not really warrant his selection

here. The photo of the grassy area containing his unmarked grave is not remarkable either. Possibly of interest is the fact that he has the 12th-most plate appearances of all time for a player with no more than one home run. My reason for including him here is the fact that his one home run came off Hall of Famer John Montgomery Ward in the bottom of the second inning on June 27, 1881.

CEDRIC DURST, EL CAMINO MEMORIAL PARK

Durst played in the majors in 1922–23, and then again in 1926–30. Most notably, he was the fourth outfielder on the 1927 "Murderers' Row" New York Yankees, behind three guys named Babe Ruth, Bob Meusel, and Earle Combs. Durst was not one of the reasons for the team's nickname, hitting exactly zero home runs in his 129 at-bats. He went 0-for-1 in the 1927 World Series but in the 1928 Series, he was 3-for-8 with a home run.

CHICO RUIZ, EL CAMINO MEMORIAL PARK

This picture of the grave marker of Ruiz shows one of the challenges of my work. Sometimes the picture is not going to be great. Some markers don't have a great contrast in colors so they can be hard to read. Others have been run over by cemetery vehicles, leaving dirt that obscures what may already be difficult engravings to read. Ruiz was not a particularly accomplished player but he played from 1964 through 1971, the years when, as a child, I first started paying attention to baseball. And for some reason, I just liked that guy named Chico Ruiz. Probably his greatest achievement in baseball occurred on September 21, 1964, playing for the Cincinnati Reds against the Philadelphia Phillies. With Frank Robinson at bat in the sixth inning, Ruiz decided to try to steal home. He was successful in scoring what turned out to be the only run of the game. And that game was the beginning of the collapse that saw the Phillies blow a 6½-game lead with just 12 games left in the season.

BILL GLYNN, FORT ROSECRANS NATIONAL CEMETERY

Glynn did not have a particularly auspicious baseball career. But he had already made a name for himself. He served in the infantry in World War II, earning the Bronze Star Medal, which is given for "heroic achievement, heroic service, meritorious achievement, or meritorious service in a combat zone." After his military service ended, he spent four years in the minors before a cup of coffee with the Phillies in 1949. He spent a little more time in the minors before getting back to the majors in 1952–54. That included one year as the Cleveland Indians' regular first baseman. His career highlight came on July 5, 1954, when he hit three home runs, narrowly missing a fourth, which would have been a grand slam, and knocked in eight runs.

JERRY COLEMAN, MIRAMAR NATIONAL CEMETERY

A California native, Jerry Coleman spent most of the 1950s as an infielder for some very good Yankees teams. He had three years where he was the regular second baseman. After his playing career ended he became a broadcaster. From 1972 to 2013, he was the lead radio broadcaster for the San Diego Padres—except in 1980, when he served one season as the Padres manager. His catchphrase, used after a nice defensive play, was "You can hang a star on that one, baby!" He was also well known for verbal bloopers. "Winfield goes back to the wall, he hits his head on the wall and it rolls off! It's rolling all the way back to second base. This is a terrible thing for the Padres."[1] "You never ask why you've been fired because if you do, they're liable to tell you," "On the mound is Randy Jones, the left-hander with the Karl Marx hairdo."

HICK CARPENTER, MOUNT HOPE CEMETERY

Hick Carpenter is another Mount Hope Cemetery unmarked grave. Unlike Quest, however, his baseball career was noteworthy. Carpenter had a couple of very good offensive seasons and, despite throwing left-handed, was a good defensive third baseman. He was frequently in league top tens in offensive categories. Likewise, his name regularly dotted fielding-statistic leaderboards, including four years leading his league in putouts.

JOAN AND RAY KROC, EL CAMINO MEMORIAL PARK

Ray Kroc became a wealthy man due to his ownership of McDonald's. He was not the founder, though he got into the game very early. Some allege that he undermined the McDonald brothers and pushed them out. In any case, he was instrumental in many innovations found in McDonald's restaurants, including a special emphasis on cleanliness. That makes those restaurants a frequent stop for us while on trips due to the high probability that the restrooms will be clean. He retired from running McDonald's in 1974 and turned his attention to baseball, a lifelong passion. The Padres were close to being moved to Washington, DC, but the sale was held up by lawsuits, giving Kroc the opportunity to buy the team for $10 million.

Upon Ray's death in 1984, his widow Joan maintained ownership after first trying to donate the team to San Diego. Major league rules prohibited that. She sold the team in 1990.

ARTHUR E MEYERHOFF (AAGPBL EXEC), EL CAMINO MEMORIAL PARK

I don't know how I found out that Meyerhoff was buried in El Camino Memorial Park. I had never heard of him. But reading his biography at the All-American Girls Professional Baseball League website (https://www.aagpbl.org/profiles/arthur-e-meyerhoff-ned/912) showed me a very interesting man. He was a businessman, an inventor, an author, and, beginning at age 80, an aspiring pilot. He started a 60-year association with the Wrigley Company in 1932 and helped Philip Wrigley start the AAGPBL. He purchased the league assets from Wrigley in 1944.

C ARNHOLT SMITH, GREENWOOD MEMORIAL PARK

Smith was the original owner of the major-league San Diego Padres. Not long after the team began playing, Smith sought to move it to Washington, eventually giving up and selling the club to the Krocs. Much of his wealth came from banking. In 1973, his bank failed and he was sued by the IRS for $23 million in back taxes. He eventually ended up in jail for tax evasion, though he was found innocent of charges connected to his sale of the Padres.[2]

RAY BOONE, EL CAMINO MEMORIAL PARK

Boone was a 13-year major-league shortstop and third baseman who was an All-Star twice and put together a very productive career. He also produced a son, Bob, and two grandsons, Aaron and Bret, who each spent more than a decade in major league baseball. He appeared in the World Series for the Indians in 1948 despite playing in only six games during his rookie year. However, he never played in another World Series. Bob, Aaron, and Bret also saw World Series action.

JACK HARSHMAN, FORT ROSECRANS NATIONAL CEMETERY

A 10-year major leaguer, Harshman came up as a first baseman but later became a pitcher. He posted double figures in wins four times. His best years were 1954, his first full season in the majors, 1956, and 1958, which saw him tally two points in the Most Valuable Player voting. He played for the New York Giants in 1950 and '52 but spent 1951 in the minors while the Giants went to the World Series. He was with the Chicago White Sox from 1954 to '57 but was gone when they went to the World Series in 1959. He was with Cleveland in 1959 and '60, having already missed their 1954 World Series trip. His initial promise as a first baseman showed itself in his hitting: He's tied for the 14th-most lifetime home runs for a pitcher, with 19 of his 21 coming in that role, including six each in 1956 and '58.

BOB ELLIOTT, GREENWOOD MEMORIAL PARK

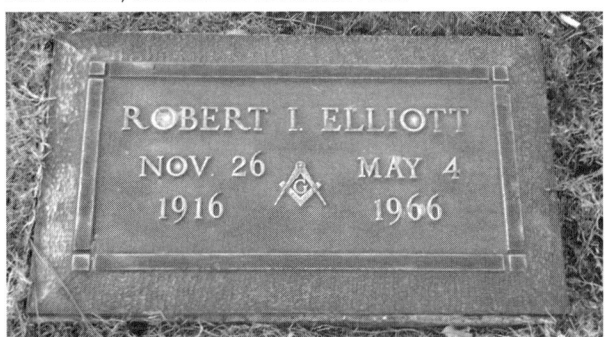

Elliott was a seven-time All-Star who was the National League Most Valuable Player in 1947. My favorite fact about Elliott is that he drew 131 walks in 1948, 41 more than he drew in any other of his 15 major-league seasons. He batted .333 with two home runs in the 1948 World Series as his Boston Braves lost to the Indians in six games. He received Hall of Fame votes three times but never came close to enshrinement, topping out at 2 percent in 1964.

BID McPHEE, CYPRESS VIEW CEMETERY & MAUSOLEUM

San Diego's only Hall of Fame grave site is Bid McPhee's. His location shows another problem when doing photographs of burial sites. His urn is behind dirty glass in a poorly lit area in an old mausoleum. McPhee played in the 1880s and '90s. He was elected to the Hall in 2000. His offensive numbers do not make him an obvious honoree. His defensive numbers, however, are impressive. He led his league in fielding percentage eight times, assists six times, putouts eight times, and double plays 11 times. Offensively he led the league in triples, games, and homers once each. ■

OTHER MAJOR LEAGUE BURIALS IN SAN DIEGO

Robert Walter "Bob" Jones	El Camino Memorial Park
Earle Francis Brucker Sr	Greenwood Memorial Park
Stephen Mathias "Steve" Mesner	Greenwood Memorial Park
Harry H Raymond	Greenwood Memorial Park
Albert James "Al" Carson	Cypress View Cemetery & Mausoleum
Roy Lee Hutson	Cypress View Cemetery & Mausoleum
William "Chick" "Bill" Starr	Cypress View Cemetery & Mausoleum
Anthony Paul "Tony" Criscola	El Camino Memorial Park
Michael Wayne "Mike" Reinbach	El Camino Memorial Park
Harold John "Jack" Albright	Fort Rosecrans National Cemetery
Earle Francis Brucker Jr	Fort Rosecrans National Cemetery
Howard Oliver Craghead	Fort Rosecrans National Cemetery
William Edgar "Bud" Hardin	Fort Rosecrans National Cemetery
Rolla Hamilton Mapel	Fort Rosecrans National Cemetery
Joseph Aloysius "Goldie" Rapp	Fort Rosecrans National Cemetery
Marvin Harold "Red" Smith	Fort Rosecrans National Cemetery
William Dunn "Bill" Dalrymple	Greenwood Memorial Park
Clarence Franklin "Lefty" Hopper	Greenwood Memorial Park
Milton Smith	Greenwood Memorial Park
Robert Joseph "Bob" Thorpe	Greenwood Memorial Park
William Thomas "Bill" Burns	Holy Cross Cemetery
Rodney Blaine "Rod" Graber	Miramar National Cemetery
Chester Lawrence "Chet" Kehn	Mount Hope Cemetery

Notes

1. https://ftw.usatoday.com/2014/01/jerry-coleman-best-quotes.
2. https://www.washingtonpost.com/archive/politics/1979/05/04/arnholt-smith-guilty-of-evading-taxes/ced41e56-552d-4568-9c19-ec04db836337/?utm_term=.0d95952666fc.

Raw Materials

The Padres' Expansion 30

Mark Camps

On October 14, 1968, just four days after the final out of the World Series, the National League held an expansion draft, allowing the two new teams who were to join the Senior Circuit the next season to bulk up their rosters with 30 "unprotected" players from the other 10 NL teams.

At the Windsor Hotel in Montreal, executives for the San Diego Padres and the Montreal Expos gathered to make their selections. The Padres said they drafted for speed, pitching, and fielding.[1] What they got was a collection of players with little or no big-league experience. The few veterans they did draft were mostly traded away for more youth.

It was an eclectic bunch. There was an American League MVP, a former member of Panama's national soccer team, and another who appeared as a guest star on *Gilligan's Island* and *Batman*. Eight were born in Latin America or the Caribbean, including three who were from Cuba—as was Padres manager Preston Gomez.

Of the 30 players taken that day, 26 played at least a few games for the 1969 club.[2] The other four were either traded before the season started or never made it to the big leagues. The oldest was 32 when he was drafted and the youngest was 19. Four became All-Stars. Another nine would go on to play on division or pennant winners—with other teams, of course.

Seventeen were still alive as of April 2019. Of the 13 that are no longer with us, three died in their 40s.[3]

Here's a thumbnail sketch of the 30 original Padres:

OLLIE BROWN: He was the first player selected in the expansion draft after the Giants, with too many outfielders, left him unprotected. Known for a cannon arm and powerful bat (he hit 40 homers for Class A Fresno in 1964), Downtown Brown hit 20 homers in 1969 and 23 in 1970. Oddly, he may not have been the best athlete in his family. One brother, Oscar, played with the Atlanta Braves and the other, Willie, was an NFL running back.[4] In a 13-year career, he reached

the postseason twice, with the Philadelphia Phillies in 1976–77, going 0-for-4 with a walk.

DAVE GIUSTI: He was one of the most accomplished players the Padres drafted, having pitched four straight solid seasons for Houston, winning 15 games in 1966. Traded by the Astros to St. Louis shortly before the expansion draft, he was left unprotected by the Cardinals, and when the Padres took him, Giusti was openly unenthusiastic about joining them.[5] The Padres obliged seven weeks later, sending him back to the Cardinals for four players, including Ed Spiezio. A key infielder for the young club, Spiezio is etched in Padres lore for collecting the first hit and home run in Padres history.

DICK SELMA: Selma's stay in San Diego was brief, but not without fanfare. After he showed flashes of brilliance with the New York Mets in 1965–68, the Padres took him and made him their Opening Day starter in 1969. He delivered the Padres' first-ever win, a 2–1, complete-game, 12-strike-out decision over the Astros. Oddly, he would make just three more appearances before he was dealt to the Chicago Cubs for three players, including Joe Niekro.

Ollie "Downtown" Brown, the Padres' first selection in the expansion draft, played 13 seasons in the majors. He was the Padres' first slugger, reaching the 20-homer mark in both 1969 and '70.

AL SANTORINI: One of the youngest players drafted by the Padres, Santorini showed the poise of a veteran in 1969, giving the fledgling club what it needed—innings and an occasional win. At age 20, he made his first start for the Padres on April 18. He got the win, and the Padres ended their six-game losing streak that day, beating the San Francisco Giants, 3–1, at Candlestick Park.[6] Santorini would make a career-high 30 starts in 1969. His eight victories were tied for most on the club.

JOSE ARCIA: A career .215 batter in almost 300 games and not much of a base stealer (caught 13 times in 30 tries), Arcia was nonetheless a valuable utility player for the 1969–70 Padres, playing all four infield positions as well as left field. In 1968, as a member of the Cubs, he delivered his only big-league homer in grand style, beating the Pittsburgh Pirates and veteran Bob Veale with a ninth-inning walk-off at Wrigley Field.

CLAY KIRBY: He's known best for the no-hitters that didn't quite happen. The most infamous was when Gomez removed him, trailing 1–0, for a pinch-hitter after eight no-hit innings against the Mets on July 21, 1970.[7] Kirby, who won 10 or more games six times, also took no-nos into the eighth inning twice in 1971. Like Santorini, Kirby was 20 when he became a full-time starter in 1969. That year he would lead the team in strikeouts and innings pitched and tie for the league lead with 20 losses.

FRED KENDALL: The last of the expansion Padres to depart the club, the talented catcher played on the first eight editions (1969–76). After playing sparingly the first four seasons and compiling a .196 batting average, Kendall finally got his chance to start full-time in 1973, and he put it all together: 10 homers, 59 RBIs, .282 batting average in 145 games. He remained the starter for the next three seasons but was dealt to the Cleveland Indians following the 1976 season. He returned to the Padres for his swan song, batting .190 in parts of 1979 and '80.

JERRY MORALES: The youngest player drafted by the Padres, Morales was 19 when he was taken from the Mets system. After three mostly minor-league seasons, he had two solid seasons at the big-league level in 1972–73 as part of an outfield platoon. His career blossomed after he was traded to the Cubs following the 1973 season. Second in the NL in batting average (.331) at the break in 1977, Morales made his only All-Star Game, scoring a run in the eighth inning.[8]

NATE COLBERT: He played in the Padres' first six seasons and he's still the team's career home run leader (163) nearly 45 years after his last at-bat. From 1968 to '76, Colbert played on nine consecutive last-place teams—one with the Astros and two with the Expos, sandwiched around six with the Padres. In August 1972, he became the second player to hit five homers in a doubleheader. As an 8-year-old growing up in St. Louis, he was in the ballpark in 1954 when Stan Musial was the first to do it.[9]

ZOILO VERSALLES: The 1965 AL MVP and World Series hero never played for San Diego as he was traded to Cleveland just seven weeks after the expansion draft. The Padres received 6-foot-7 Bill Davis, who was their starting first baseman in their first game, going 0-for-3. However, Davis amassed just 57 at-bats with San Diego before being dealt to the Cardinals in late May. He never played in the majors again.

FRANK REBERGER: He appeared in a team-high 67 games for the Padres in 1969, good for fifth in the league and a team record that stood for five years. Despite his durability, he was sent to the Giants following the '69 season for three players: Bob Barton, Bobby Etheridge, and Ron Herbel. Splitting his time as a starter and a reliever with the Giants in 1970, Reberger tossed

Nearly 45 years after his last at-bat with the Padres, Nate Colbert is still the club leader with 163 career home runs. Five were hit in one day, a double-header in August 1972.

NATIONAL BASEBALL HALL OF FAME AND LIBRARY, COOPERSTOWN, NY

a 10-inning complete game in San Diego, beating his former mates, 3–2.

JERRY DAVANON: A local boy (born in Oceanside), DaVanon made 12 starts at shortstop and second base for the 1969 Padres before he was benched and eventually traded to the Cardinals in late May. In 1971, DaVanon was a backup infielder on the pennant-winning Baltimore Orioles but did not appear in a postseason game. His son, Jeff, played eight years in the majors, mostly with the Anaheim/Los Angeles Angels.

LARRY STAHL: In a rather unremarkable career, Stahl had one of the most infamous bases on balls in history.[10] A fixture on the Padres' early rosters (1969–72), Stahl was the 27th batter in what might have been a perfect game for Milt Pappas of the Cubs. Stahl fell behind 1–2 and then took three straight close pitches that the home plate umpire called balls. Pappas secured his no-hitter by retiring the next batter, Garry Jestadt.

DICK KELLEY: Arguably the top performer in the '69 Padres' starting rotation, the left-handed Kelley led the staff with a 3.57 ERA, fewest hits per nine innings, and most strikeouts per nine, despite winning just four times in 23 starts. He spun the best game of his career on July 6, one-hitting the Astros, the lone hit coming on an infield single. Limited by arm and shoulder injuries, he compiled an 18–30 career record.

AL FERRARA: Left unprotected by the Dodgers, Ferrara delivered as the Padres' left fielder, hitting 27 homers over the first two seasons while batting .268. Somewhat of a bon vivant during his time with the Dodgers (1963, 1965–68), he had guest appearances on TV shows such as *Gilligan's Island* and *Batman*.[11] With the Dodgers, he was a member of three World Series rosters (1963, '65, '66) but didn't get into a game until the final inning of the 1966 Series against the Orioles. In the ninth inning of Game 4, Ferrara collected a pinch-single, one of just 17 hits the Dodgers would get in the entire Series.

MIKE CORKINS: Corkins spent his entire six-year big league career (1969–74) with the Padres, winning 18 games. Corkins did a little bit of everything, from being a member of the starting rotation in

1970 to the team leader in saves, with six, in 1972. He achieved some notoriety both for hitting and yielding home runs. His first of five career homers was a grand slam off 20-game winner Jim Merritt of the Cincinnati Reds in 1970. On the flipside, Willie Mays tagged him for No. 600 in 1969.[12]

TOM DUKES: After the 1970 season, in which he led the club in saves (10) and was second in appearances (53), Dukes was part of a trade that turned out to be one-sided, and not in the Padres' favor. He and Pat Dobson, a 14-game winner in 1970, were sent to the Orioles for four players. Dobson won 20 games the next season for the AL pennant winners and Dukes responded with his finest statistical season. In the Orioles' seven-game Series loss to the Pirates, Dukes pitched four scoreless innings of relief.

RICK JAMES: Perhaps the best athlete ever to come out of Coffee High School in Florence, Alabama, James had a cup of coffee in the bigs, and that was it. The first-ever first-round pick by the Cubs (No. 6 overall in the inaugural amateur draft in 1965), James was 19 years old when he got into his only three major league games, tossing 4 innings, all in 1967. He was selected by the Padres but remained in the minors in 1969 and '70. He was out of baseball after that, before turning 23.

TONY GONZALEZ: One of the few proven hitters drafted by the Padres and the oldest (32), Gonzalez received MVP votes three times in the 1960s and was second in the NL in batting average (.339) in 1967. With the 1969 Padres, he batted just .225 in 53 games. He was traded to the Braves in June 1969 for three players (including future hitting guru Walt Hriniak), but the Braves got the better of the deal. Gonzalez hit 10 homers down the stretch as Atlanta won the NL West. Gonzalez stood out in the League Championship Series, batting .357 in 14 at-bats against the Mets, including a homer and double off Tom Seaver in Game One. It would be his only postseason appearance.

DAVE ROBERTS: Between 1962 and 2008, four men named Dave Roberts played in the majors, but this Dave Roberts was the best—and only—pitcher. Drafted from the Pirates, Roberts made

60 starts for the Padres in 1969–71, and in 1971 his 2.10 ERA was second in the NL. Dealt to the Astros after the '71 season, Roberts cemented his reputation as one of the era's sturdiest hurlers by compiling 52 complete games and 15 shutouts in 1972–76. In 1979, Roberts (who played for eight teams during his career) rejoined the Pirates and won a World Series ring, pitching out of the bullpen.

IVAN MURRELL: A multisport star (boxing, soccer, baseball) in his native Panama, Murrell played 10 years with the Colt .45s/Astros, Padres and Braves.[13] He was a mainstay in the Padres' outfield in 1970, collecting career bests in home runs (12), RBIs (35), hits (85), and games played (125). Placed on waivers after the 1973 season, Murrell was picked up by the Braves and had the good fortune of watching first-hand as Henry Aaron broke Babe Ruth's home run record.

JIM WILLIAMS: Drafted by the Cubs out of Ells High School in Richmond, California—the same school that produced Gene Clines and Willie McGee, Williams was traded to the Dodgers in 1967 before being selected by the Padres. In 1969, Williams showed great speed in the minors, stealing 26 bags in 31 tries before his September call-up. In the majors, he batted .280 in 13 games but didn't attempt a steal. After a September call-up the next year, Williams played three more seasons in the minors but never played in the bigs again.

BILLY McCOOL: Blessed with a live left arm, McCool was a can't-miss who didn't live up to the hype, largely because of injuries. He was 19 when he made his debut for the Reds in 1964, and he was an All-Star in 1966. After two subpar years in 1967 and '68, he was left unprotected by the Reds and the Padres took him. Shoulder and foot injuries derailed most of his 1969 season with San Diego, although he did make 54 appearances, all in relief. The McCool experiment ended for the Padres when they dealt him to St. Louis shortly before the 1970 season.

ROBERTO PEÑA: After spending most of the 1960s trying to hook on with the Pirates, Cubs, and Phillies organizations, Peña looked like he'd found a home in San Diego after he batted .250 in more than 500 plate appearances in 1969 while playing all four infield positions. But before the 1970 season began, Peña was traded again, this time to the Oakland A's for backup outfielder Ramon Webster. Less than two months later, Pena was dealt once more, this time to the Milwaukee Brewers. After the 1971 season, at age 34, he played three years in the Mexican League before hanging up his spikes for good.

AL McBEAN: Left unprotected by the Pirates after eight solid seasons split between starting and relieving, the 30-year-old McBean was taken by the Padres and made just one appearance, a seven-inning start against the Giants in the fifth game of the 1969 season.[14] A week later, he was dealt to the Dodgers for backup infielder Tommy Dean and a little-used reliever named Leon Everitt. McBean would return to the Pirates in 1970 before retiring. He pitched on several playoff-contending teams during his 10-year career but never appeared in the postseason, having the misfortune of playing for the Pirates the year after they won the World Series (1961) and the year before (1970).

RAFAEL ROBLES: Robles was the first player to come to bat for the Padres. On April 8, 1969, he led off the bottom of the first inning against the Astros' Don Wilson. Robles reached on an error by Hall of Fame second baseman Joe Morgan, then stole second base, but did not score. He started the first six games of the season, went 2-for-20 at the plate and was banished to the minors for the rest of the season. His soft hitting would continue throughout his career, as he had just one extra-base hit in 133 at-bats. Robles would remain in the Padres organization until June 1972, when he was traded to St. Louis.

FRED KATAWCZIK: Taken from the Reds organization, Katawczik was the only one of the 30 players the Padres took in the expansion draft who never played in the majors. The 6-foot-4 left hander reached Triple-A for both the Reds in 1968 and the Padres in 1970 but couldn't crack the big clubs. He gave up baseball after the 1970 season at age 21.[15]

RON SLOCUM: After taking Slocum from the Pirates, the Padres had designs of turning the hometown boy into their everyday catcher, but his difficulties hitting at the big-league level (career .150

batting average in 80 games) derailed those plans.[16] In three seasons in a utility role, he nonetheless had several memorable moments, including a three-run homer off former Cy Young award winner Mike McCormick of the Giants in a wild 17–16, 15-inning win in 1970.

STEVE ARLIN: A workhorse for the Padres, he went 19–40 in 1971–72 and is still the only pitcher in the past 50 seasons to lose at least 40 games over a two-season span. He's come the closest of any Padres pitcher to throwing a no-hitter, losing one to the Phillies with two outs in the ninth inning on June 18, 1972. Before the Phillies took him with their first pick in the 1966 draft, 13th overall, Arlin was one of the finest college pitchers ever, going 24–3 over two years at Ohio State. Arlin's College World Series résumé included a 20-strikeout, 15-inning win in 1965 and a Most Outstanding Player trophy in 1966. His grandfather, Harold, is credited as the first broadcaster ever to call a game on the radio, in 1921.[17]

CITO GASTON: Before he was renowned for winning back-to-back World Series in 1992 and '93 as the manager of the Toronto Blue Jays, this little-known Braves farmhand was the Padres' final pick of the expansion draft. A one-time roommate of Aaron, Gaston was a fixture in the Padres' outfield in 1969–74.[18] His 11-year big-league career peaked in 1970 when he made his only All-Star team en route to a .318/29/93 season. His managerial career easily surpassed his accomplishments as a player: He won 894 games in two stints as Toronto's skipper. Gaston was enshrined in the Canadian Baseball Hall of Fame in 2002.[19] ∎

NATIONAL BASEBALL HALL OF FAME AND LIBRARY, COOPERSTOWN, NY

Long before he became a highly successful manager, Cito Gaston was the Padres' final pick in the expansion draft, and he turned out to be one of their best. In 1970, he was an All-Star, hitting .318 with 29 home runs.

Notes

1. John Bauer, "It's a Major League City or It Isn't: San Diego's Padres Step Up to the Big Leagues," in *Time for Expansion Baseball*, ed. Maxwell Kates and Bill Nowlin (Phoenix, SABR, 2018), 195–203.
2. Joe Lanek, "Ollie Brown headlined the Padres' expansion draft selections this day in 1968," Gaslamp Ball, October 14, 2014. https://www.gaslampball.com/2014/10/14/6972151/padres-expansion-draft-1968-ollie-brown-cito-gaston.
3. The 13 who have died are Ollie Brown, Dick Selma, Jose Arcia, Clay Kirby, Zoilo Versalles, Dick Kelley, Dave Roberts, Ivan Murrell, Billy McCool, Roberto Peña, Rafael Robles, Ron Slocum, and Steve Arlin. Kirby, Peña, and Slocum died in their 40s.
4. Gary Klein, "Ollie 'Downtown' Brown, baseball's 'Original Padre,' dies at 71," *Los Angeles Times*, May 15, 2015.
5. Bauer, "It's a Major League City or It Isn't."
6. Except as noted, the source for all statistics, results, and transactions is Baseball-Reference.com.
7. "Padres Near No-Hitters," Nonohitters.com. https://www.nonohitters.com/padres-near-no-hitters/.
8. Bauer, "It's a Major League City or It Isn't."
9. Bauer.
10. George Castle, "Possible balky CF camera gives no peace to Pappas for blown '72 perfect game," (Northwest Indiana) *Times*, September 4, 2012. https://www.nwitimes.com/sports/baseball/professional/mlb/cubs/possible-balky-cf-camera-gives-no-peace-to-pappas-for/article_3194b96e-01d6-5d71-82cb-e6a28e4bcb01.html.
11. Paul Hirsch, "Al Ferrara," SABR BioProject. https://sabr.org/bioproj/person/2de64825.
12. "Mays Blasts 600th!" *Sarasota Herald Tribune*, September 24, 1969. https://news.google.com/newspapers?nid=1755&dat=19690924&id=_j8eAAAAIBAJ&sjid=YL8EAAAAIBAJ&pg=6172,6672757&hl=en.
13. "In Memory of Ivan Murrell," *The Treasure Coast Palm*, October 11, 2016. http://www.astrosdaily.com/players/obits/Murrell_Ivan.html; Sandy Burgin, "Where Have You Gone, Ivan Murrell?" MLB.com, date unknown. Both via Astros Daily. http://www.astrosdaily.com/players/obits/Murrell_Ivan.html.
14. Geoff Young, *Duck Snorts 2009 Baseball Annual* (Lulu.com, 2009), 172.
15. Young.
16. Bauer, "It's a Major League City or It Isn't."
17. Jeff Sanders, "Former Padres RHP Steve Arlin dies at 70," *San Diego Union-Tribune*, August 22, 2016. https://www.sandiegouniontribune.com/sdut-padres-pitcher-steve-arlin-dies-2016aug22-story.html; "Buckeyes Nip Cougars Nine, Battle Arizona St. in Finals," *Spokane Daily Chronicle*, June 11, 1965. https://news.google.com/newspapers?id=cFdYAAAAIBAJ&sjid=n_cDAAAAIBAJ&pg=5691%2C2817691; "Most Outstanding Player Award in College World Series," Baseball Almanac. http://www.baseball-almanac.com/awards/most_outstanding_player_award.shtml.
18. Alfonso L Tusa C, "Cito Gaston," SABR BioProject. https://sabr.org/bioproj/person/946b8db1.
19. Walter Leavy, "Cito Gaston: on top of the baseball world," *Ebony*, May 1994. https://books.google.com/books?id=1HhtOl8Lw7EC&pg=PA144&source=gbs_toc_r&cad=2#v=onepage&q&f=false.

San Diego Padres Near No-Hitters

Steven M. Glassman

In 7,976 regular-season games through the end of the 2018 season, the San Diego Padres had never thrown a no-hitter.[1] Five times, the Padres have taken no-hit bids into the ninth inning. Here are summaries of those games, with the date, pitcher(s), opponent, and location.

July 21, 1970 – Clay Kirby and Jack Baldschun
8 innings vs. New York Mets, San Diego Stadium

Kirby entered the contest with a 5.03 earned run average, third-worst in the National League.[2] He'd pitched twice against the Mets that season (April 21 at Shea Stadium and May 2 in San Diego), throwing a total of 13 innings, allowing six runs on 10 hits.

Kirby allowed his only run in the first inning. Tommy Agee led off with a walk and stole second. One out later, Ken Singleton also walked. Agee and Singleton pulled off a double steal with Art Shamsky at bat, and Agee scored on Shamsky's groundout to second baseman Ron Slocum. Kirby retired the Mets in order from the second through fourth innings, retiring 12 straight hitters before Joe Foy walked with one out in the fifth. He also walked Adrian Garrett with two outs in the seventh. Kirby allowed a leadoff walk in the eighth to Joe Foy, who stole second but was out at home on a Jim McAndrew fielder's choice to Nate Colbert.

This game would be remembered for Padres manager Preston Gomez's decision to pinch-hit for Kirby with two out in the eighth and the Mets still leading, 1–0. Kirby was in the on-deck circle while Bob Barton was at bat against McAndrew. Gomez called Kirby back to the dugout and replaced him with Cito Gaston, who was usually a starter but had sat out with a strained leg muscle.[3] "The Mets bench just gasped in disbelief," Tom Seaver said. "I personally would have let him hit. If the pennant race was involved, no. But in this situation, yes."[4] The decision was met with boos and the reaction got worse when Gaston, pinch-hitting for the first time all year, struck out swinging.

Gomez replaced Kirby with Baldschun to start the ninth. Bud Harrelson lined Baldschun's fourth pitch to left for the Mets' first hit.[5] The game was briefly interrupted when a fan went into the Padres dugout and was removed by police. Singleton sacrificed Harrelson to second. Shamsky was intentionally walked and was pinch-run for by Mike Jorgensen. Cleon Jones's single to right loaded the bases. Baldschun struck out Garrett but Foy's two-out single to left scored Harrelson and Jorgensen to make it 3–0.

Gomez's decision to remove Kirby was met with mixed postgame reactions from both organizations and around baseball. Padres President Buzzie Bavasi wanted Kirby to stay in the game. He said, "I want to win more than anybody and I don't second-guess him. But it's once in a lifetime for the kid."[6] Gomez stood by his decision. "It would have been the easy way for me to let the kid go up and hit," Gomez said. "I don't play for the fans. I play to win. In fact, if Ed Spiezio had led off the eighth with a hit, I would have bunted him over to second and then pinch-hit for the pitcher. I did the same thing in Spokane by taking Phil Ortega out after seven innings and we eventually won the game."[7] In *The Sporting News*, Paul Cour wrote that "at first, Kirby was visibly disturbed at being denied the chance to make the record book, but, by the time he met the press, he was calm and gracious."[8]

"I was a little surprised," Kirby said, "but he's the manager and he has to make a decision. I'm only 22 and I'll have plenty of time to pitch a no-hitter."[9] Kirby added: "Everyone wants to pitch a no-hitter and I was so close."[10] Mets broadcaster Ralph Kiner—once a general manager of the Pacific Coast League Padres—and New York Yankees manager Ralph Houk also agreed with Gomez. Jerome Holtzman wrote in *The Sporting News* that Gomez "revealed that he received

Clayton Laws Kirby Jr. was one of the original players taken by the Padres in the expansion draft.

a letter from Al Lopez, the former White Sox pilot. Lopez congratulated Gomez on his decision to lift Clay Kirby, even though Kirby had a no-hitter going. Al wrote, 'What you did shows courage and besides, it was the best thing to do.'" According to Cour, "Within seconds of Gomez's decision, the Padres and newspaper switchboards were swamped with calls. Most of the callers were yelling for Gomez's scalp."

"I would never second-guess myself," Gomez said. "And I can always go home after a game and sleep, figuring I did what I thought was right."[12]

July 18, 1972 – Steve Arlin
8⅔ innings vs. Philadelphia Phillies, San Diego Stadium

Arlin was facing the team that drafted him 13th overall in the June 1966 secondary phase of the Amateur Free Agent Draft. However, the Phillies left him unprotected and the Padres drafted him 57th in the 1968 National League Expansion Draft. Entering this game, he'd started against the Phillies four times, posting a 2.15 ERA in 29⅓ innings and holding his former organization to a .187 batting average.

He got run support in the first inning from a two-out RBI double to left by Colbert off Bill Champion. That scored Jerry Morales, who had walked. The Padres struck again in the fifth with Colbert's two-run home run and in the seventh when they scored twice more in a rally highlighted by Morales's triple and Gaston's double.

In the first eight innings, Arlin allowed walks to Tom Hutton (two out in the first), Willie Montanez (none out in the fifth), and Larry Bowa (two out in the sixth).[13] Doyle nearly broke up the no-hit bid in the sixth with two outs, but, as the *Philadelphia Inquirer*'s Bruce Keidan described it, "Padre second baseman Derrel Thomas absconded with it. Thomas raced to his right, dived and somehow came up with the sharply hit grounder. Then still lying on his back, he threw the ball to Colbert in time to nip Doyle at first base for the third out of the sixth inning." In the ninth, Deron Johnson, pinch-hitting for reliever Wayne Twitchell, lined out to third baseman Dave Roberts. After Bowa made the second out, "Doyle chopped a 1–2 pitch into the grass and raced to first as the ball bounced into left field. Arlin then lost his shutout by balking Doyle to second and giving up his second and last hit, a single to right by Tommy Hutton."[14] Arlin finished the game, retiring Greg Luzinski on a fly out to Johnny Jeter.[15]

Padres' first-year San Diego manager Don Zimmer took responsibility for Doyle breaking up Arlin's no-hit bid in the ninth. "I messed it up," he said. "Doyle's primarily a pull hitter, and I didn't want him just topping a ball and beating out a swinging bunt. Roberts was playing shallow on Doyle. He wanted to move back after Arlin got two strike[s] on him. I made Roberts stay in close. If I had let him move back, he would have fielded the ball." Roberts's reaction: "I'm sick, I'm just sick."[16] Phil Collier wrote in *The Sporting News* that "when Arlin returned to the clubhouse after telling of his two-hitter on a postgame radio show, Zimmer approached him and handed him a razor blade. 'Here,' the manager said, pointing to his throat. 'Just make it quick.'"[17]

September 5, 1997 – Andy Ashby
8+ innings vs. Atlanta Braves, Qualcomm Stadium

Ashby had faced the Braves on April 26 at Atlanta-Fulton County Stadium, allowing five hits and one run in eight innings in a no-decision. This day he allowed runners to reach base in the first (Jeff Blauser on Ken Caminiti's error with one out), second (Ryan Klesko lead-off walk), and sixth (walks to Tom Glavine with one out and Blauser with two). Ashby received defensive help in the fourth from first baseman Archi Cianfrocco on a Chipper Jones groundball and helped himself on a Fred McGriff groundball to end the inning. He also got some defensive support from shortstop Craig Shipley in the fifth when "he speared a one-hop, top-spin smash struck by Javy Lopez and from his knees, threw him out for the final out in the fifth," wrote Tom Krasovic in the *San Diego Union-Tribune*. "That's when I started thinking" no-hitter, said manager Bruce Bochy.[18]

Ashby received his offensive support on a two-out Caminiti single off Glavine that scored Steve Finley in the first. Caminiti hit his 22nd home run of the season to right with one out in the third. Carlos Hernandez hit his third home run of the season with one out in the fourth. The Padres broke the game open in the seventh, scoring three and knocking Glavine out of the game.

Andy Ashby took a no-hit bid into the ninth inning only to have it broken up by Kenny Lofton. Ashby had his best years with the Padres and was part of the 1998 NL championship team.

SAN DIEGO PADRES

Kenny Lofton led off the ninth for the Braves. "I'd already been a victim of a no-hitter," the Atlanta center fielder said. "I didn't really want to do that again." Noting that Ashby was "painting the corners," Lofton said, "It was one of those nights where it all falls into place," adding, "I thought this was going to be the second time I was no-hit—Jim Abbott and Andy Ashby." Ashby's first pitch was a called strike and Lofton fouled off the next two. He then took three straight breaking balls outside for a full count. "All I was trying to do was make contact," Lofton said. Ashby's next pitch was a changeup and Lofton hit it toward Gwynn in right. "When I hit it, I knew it was going to be tailing away from Tony Gwynn," said Lofton. "But they had made great catches of balls hit like that all night." Lofton said he thought the ball might be caught at first, but then he realized Gwynn had no chance.

"I had to fight him," Lofton said. "No one wants to be among the last outs of a no-hitter. I had been fighting him all game. He was painting the corners and throwing those good sliders for strikes." Blauser flied out to Finley and Chipper Jones struck out swinging. McGriff's 21st home run of the season to right-center broke the shutout. "I don't know what I hit," said McGriff. "I was just trying to concentrate. That was the best I've felt hitting in a long time."[19] Klesko grounded out to Shipley to end the game. Wally Joyner, who made the game-ending putout, gave Ashby the game ball.

The Braves extolled Ashby's performance after the game. Braves hitters and manager Bobby Cox talked about his command, first-pitch strikes, breaking pitches, and pace on the mound.[20] They also mentioned the Padres' fielding.

September 22, 2006 – Chris Young
8⅔ innings vs. Pittsburgh Pirates, Petco Park

Young was making his next-to-last start of the season in his first year with the Padres.[21] He'd pitched well in his previous start against the Pirates on June 4 in Pittsburgh, holding them hitless for 5⅓ innings before allowing a Jose Hernandez single to left. He also allowed a one-out Jason Bay triple to center in the seventh. Altogether, Young allowed two hits and a walk in eight innings and got credit for the 1–0 victory.

On September 22, Young picked up where he left off against the Pirates. He retired the first 17 hitters before allowing a two-out walk to pinch-hitter Rajai Davis in the sixth. Davis was caught stealing second when he slid past the bag.[22] According to the *San Diego Union-Tribune*'s Jay Posner, "The best play was made in the first inning. Jack Wilson hit a long fly ball to left field that he thought was a sure double, but

Ben Johnson caught it just as he slammed into the fence. Johnson later made a routine catch on Freddy Sanchez's fly ball to the warning track. Also, second baseman Josh Barfield caught a line drive by Xavier Nady in the second and right fielder Brian Giles snagged two line drives, one by Wilson in the seventh and the other by Ryan Doumit in the ninth."[23]

The Padres scored their first run off Tom Gorzelanny in the first inning on a one-out Mike Cameron sacrifice fly to center that scored Barfield. Adrian Gonzalez's 24th home run of the season scored Cameron with two outs in the third inning. Todd Walker added on to the lead with his ninth home run of the season with one out in the sixth off relief pitcher Brian Rogers.[24] The Padres finished off their scoring with another two-out rally in the seventh. Mike Piazza tripled to center off Rogers. Gonzalez greeted Juan Perez with a single to left that scored Piazza. Johnson followed with the Padres' second triple of the inning (to center), which scored Gonzalez.

Young entered the ninth inning with 82 pitches thrown and scheduled to face the Pirates' bottom third of the order: Doumit, Bautista, and a pinch-hitter for Jonah Bayliss. Doumit lined out to Giles for the first out. Bautista walked on six pitches. Former Padre Joe Randa pinch-hit for Bayliss and took three straight balls, then took a fastball down the middle for a called strike.[25] *North County Times* writer Brian Hiro wrote that Randa "worked the count to 3–1 before ripping an 89-mph fastball, Young's 94th pitch."[26]

"As a pinch-hitter you just try to have a good at-bat and try to hit the ball hard," said Randa, who did just that, slamming Young's fastball an estimated 421 feet onto the walkway above the fence in center field.[27] Young struck out Chris Duffy looking and walked Wilson. Bochy removed him after 107 pitches and 8⅔ innings pitched.[28] The *Union-Tribune's* Bill Center wrote, "As Bochy took the ball, he said 'great game.' Young responded by saying 'thank you.' As he walked toward the Padres dugout, he tipped his cap to the reported 40,077-strong crowd who gave him a thunderous ovation. 'My ears are still ringing,' Young said 20 minutes later. 'When I tipped my cap, I had chills.'"[29] Cla Meredith struck out Sanchez swinging to end the game.

July 9, 2011 – Aaron Harang, Josh Spence, Chad Qualls, Mike Adams, and Luke Gregerson
8⅔ innings vs. Los Angeles Dodgers, Dodger Stadium[30]

Harang had won his previous start against the Dodgers, allowing two runs and three hits in six innings in a 7–2 victory at Petco Park. He was making his first start since June 9, having suffered a stress fracture to the third metatarsal bone in his right foot.[31] Harang allowed consecutive two-out walks to Andre Ethier and Matt Kemp before James Loney popped out to Jason Bartlett to end the first inning. He allowed another walk to Tony Gywnn Jr. with one out in the third. Gwynn was caught stealing by Rob Johnson with Rafael Furcal at bat. Harang did not allow another base runner to reach for the remainder of his six innings. He walked three. He was removed after 95 pitches by manager Bud Black and was replaced by left-handed reliever Spence. "We were joking in the dugout," Harang said of Black. "He said, 'I've never had to do this,' so I said, 'Well, don't do it.' He grinned, and I knew why he did it."[32] Harang noted that Black was looking out for his health. "I think if it was a different situation and I got through seven, it's probably going to be different," he said.[33] Spence struck out left-handed hitter Ethier to start the seventh and was replaced by the right-hander Qualls. Kemp reached on a Bartlett error and Loney was intentionally walked. Qualls retired Juan Uribe on a popout to Chase Headley and got Dioner Navarro to ground out to him to end the seventh.

Adams was the Padres' fourth pitcher. He walked Jamey Carroll to lead off the eighth and Trent Oeltjen reached on Headley's error on a sacrifice bunt attempt. Adams got out of the inning on a Gwynn bunt popout to Johnson, a Furcal fly out to Chris Denorfia, and an Ethier groundout to Orlando Hudson.

Harang's mound opponent, Rubby De La Rosa, limited the Padres to one hit and four walks in six innings. Dodger relievers Matt Guerrier, Mike MacDougal, and Blake Hawksworth did not allow any Padre base runners for the remainder of the game.

Gregerson started the ninth, the fifth Padres pitcher in a scoreless tie. He was scheduled to face the middle of the Dodgers order: Kemp, Loney, and Uribe. Gregerson struck out Kemp swinging and got Loney to ground out to Rizzo unassisted to start the inning. He got ahead of Uribe in the count, 1–2, on sliders. The *Union-Tribune*'s Center wrote that "Gregerson admitted hanging a slider to Uribe, who rocketed a liner over left fielder Denorfia's head. 'I was a full stride from it,' said Denorfia."[34] After Uribe's double, Gregerson fell behind Navarro on three straight sliders before throwing a four-seam fastball for a called strike. Center wrote that Gregerson's next pitch to Navarro "was right where he wanted it, a slider low and away. But the Dodgers catcher poked it to right, the ball dropping in front of [Will] Venable's desperate charge, for a walk-off single." Gregerson responded about a

possible combined no-hitter, "Who cares? It doesn't matter at that point. I don't think anyone in the bullpen knew there was a no-hitter going." He added: "It's only fun if the starter goes nine innings and throws a no-hitter and your guys score some runs."[36] ■

Box scores courtesy of Baseball Reference, Retrosheet and MLB.com.

Notes

1. The New York Mets went 8,019 regular-season games before their first no-hitter, by Johan Santana on June 1, 2012. The Philadelphia Phillies went from May 3, 1906, to June 20, 1964, between no-hitters (8,936 regular-season games). The Cleveland Indians hold the American League mark between no-hitters (6,003). Their last no-hitter was Len Barker's perfect game versus the Toronto Blue Jays on May 15, 1981. The Detroit Tigers went from July 5, 1912, to May 14, 1952, between no-hitters (5,561). It is not known which team holds the AL record for games without a no-hitter from the start of its franchise. https://www.nonohitters.com/.

2. Montreal Expo Bill Stoneman (5.33) and San Francisco Giant Juan Marichal (5.30) had worse ERAs than Kirby entering that day. https://www.retrosheet.org/boxesetc/1970/DL07201970.htm.

3. Joe Durso, "Mets Beat Padres 3-0, Despite Being Held Hitless by Kirby for 8 Innings," *The New York Times*, July 22, 1970.

4. Durso, "8 inning No-Hitter Irks Fans on Coast," *The New York Times*, July 23, 1970.

5. Durso, "Mets Beat Padres 3–0."

6. Durso.

7. Durso, "8 inning No-Hitter Irks Fans on Coast."

8. Paul Cour, "Clay Cool in Heat of No-Hit Fuss," *The Sporting News*, August 8, 1970.

9. Durso, "Mets Beat Padres 3–0."

10. Cour, "Clay Cool in Heat of No-Hit Fuss."

11. Jerome Holtzman, "Jerome Holtzman," *The Sporting News*, September 5, 1970.

12. Paul Cour, "Second-Guessers Pouring It on Poor Preston," *The Sporting News*, August 8, 1970.

13. Arlin entered the game leading the NL with 77 walks He was tied with California Angels pitcher Nolan Ryan for the major-league lead. https://www.retrosheet.org/boxesetc/1972/DL07171972.htm.

14. Bruce Keidan, "Doyle Ruins Arlin's No-Hitter in 9th," *The Philadelphia Inquirer*, July 19, 1972: 25.

15. Between June 18 and July 18, 1972, Arlin allowed two or fewer hits five times in eight starts. He allowed two hits in a complete-game win at Pittsburgh June 18; one in a complete-game win vs. San Francisco June 24; one in a 10-inning no-decision at New York July 6; two in a complete-game loss vs. New York July 14; and two in a complete-game win vs. Philadelphia July 18.

16. Sam Goldpaper, "Personalities: Pilot's Beau Geste," *The New York Times*, July 20, 1972.

17. Phil Collier, "Low-Hit Gems Are Arlin's Specialty," *The Sporting News*, August 5, 1972.

18. Tom Krasovic, "A near n000-000-000 (no) hitter for Ashby," *San Diego Union-Tribune*, September 6, 1997.

19. Bill Center, "The Fateful Ninth: Braves Lofton didn't want to be no-hit victim again," *San Diego Union-Tribune*, September 6, 1997.

20. "Working an excellent curveball that he kept low and on the corner all game, Ashby threw firstpitch strikes to 23 of the 32 batters he faced." Thomas Stinson, "Ashby pitches near no-hitter," *Atlanta Journal* and *Atlanta Constitution*, September 7, 1997.

21. Young also entered the game with the third-lowest batting average allowed in the NL and fourth in MLB (.217). His .297 on-base percentage allowed was fourth in the NL and seventh in MLB, according to Fagraphs.

22. Bill Center, "It's a One-Hit Wonder," *San Diego Union-Tribune*, September 23, 2006.

23. Jay Posner, "In a pinch, Randa jolts Young from dream game," *San Diego Union-Tribune*, September 23, 2006.

24. This was Walker's 107th and last career home run.

25. Dejan Kovacevic, "One-Hit Wonder," *Pittsburgh Post-Gazette*, September 23, 2006.

26. Brian Hiro. "Young flirts, keeps team in first," *North County Times* (Escondido, CA), September 23, 2006.

27. Posner, "In a pinch." It was also Randa's first and only career pinch-hit home run.

28. This was Young's longest outing of the 2006 season. He previously threw eight innings in consecutive starts against Colorado (May 30) and Pittsburgh (June 4).

29. Center, "It's a One-Hit Wonder."

30. There were nine combined no-hitters before the 2011 season. The most recent one at the time was on June 11, 2003, by Houston Astros pitchers Roy Oswalt, Peter Munro, Kirk Saarloos, Brad Lidge, Octavio Dotel, and Billy Wagner against the New York Yankees in Yankee Stadium.

31. Bill Center, "Near No-Hitter Goes Nowhere," *San Diego Union-Tribune*, July 10, 2011.

32. Jill Painter. "L.A. Goes From Zero to Won," *Daily News of Los Angeles*, July 10, 2011.

33. Jim Alexander, "No-hit until ninth, LA pulls it out," *Press-Enterprise* (Riverside, CA), July 10, 2011.

34. Center, "Near No-Hitter Goes Nowhere."

35. Painter, L.A. Goes From Zero to Won."

36. Center, "Near No-Hitter Goes Nowhere."

Profiles in Plumage

The San Diego Chicken

John Racanelli

June 29, 1979, was a night unlike any other at San Diego Stadium. Fans were gnarled in a four-mile-long traffic jam and the start of the game was delayed 36 minutes.[1] Gaylord Perry was scheduled to face Houston's Joaquin Andujar that night. But the capacity crowd of 47,022 was not necessarily there to see baseball.[2] San Diegans had flocked to the ballpark to watch a man hatch from a gigantic Styrofoam egg in what would become perhaps the greatest promotion in the history of baseball—the "Grand Hatching." The tale of Ted Giannoulas and his chicken suit is a quintessential study in perseverance, innovation, and, perhaps regrettably, an inexhaustible supply of barnyard puns. The Chicken's favorite baseball play, for example, is the balk.[3] With this in mind, the author has endeavored to avoid laying an egg in the telling of the San Diego Chicken's story.[4]

THE YOUNG CLUCK

Ted Giannoulas was born in London, Ontario, to parents John and Helen, who had immigrated to Canada from Greece. As a child, Ted was a rabid baseball fan and would often listen to ball games on a transistor radio hidden under his pillow, receiving AM transmissions from as far away as St. Louis, Pittsburgh, New York, and Cincinnati.[5] He organized sandlot baseball games and would bribe the best players to join his team with six-packs of soda he would sneak from his parents' restaurant. Giannoulas dreamed of someday playing shortstop for the Giants, having become a fan of the team—based some 2,500 miles from his home—when San Francisco got off to a hot start in 1962.[6]

In 1969, the Giannoulas family moved to San Diego, his father finding the agreeable weather reminiscent of his native Athens. Ted attended Hoover High School, Ted Williams's alma mater, where he was the sports editor for the school newspaper, but not the mascot. He eschewed portraying the Hoover Cardinal, joking with his friends that he was "way too cool" to be a glorified cheerleader.

After graduation, Giannoulas enrolled at San Diego State, where he majored in journalism, aspired to a career in broadcasting, and was a backup goalie for the Aztecs' club hockey team. In fact, he often ponders whether he would have ever become the Chicken if he'd been the starter.[7]

KGB RADIO AND THE RISE OF THE CHICKEN

Giannoulas becoming the Chicken was mere happenstance. While he was hanging out at San Diego State right before spring break, a man from KGB radio approached a group of students and asked if anyone was interested in passing out eggs at the San Diego Zoo for a radio promotion—a job that was to last two weeks and pay $2 an hour.[8] Giannoulas, who was 5'3" and 120 pounds "flopping wet," was chosen as the one most likely to fit the rented chicken costume.[9] He saw the chicken job as a foot in the door for future employment in KGB's news department.[10]

Giannoulas attended the Padres home opener on April 9, 1974, dressed in the chicken costume, mainly so he could get in free.[11] KGB told him, "Just be a fan. Buy a beer and a hot dog, cheer on the Padres."[12] So that was what Giannoulas did, along with shaking hands and kissing babies. He left the game early, but not before new Padres owner Ray Kroc grabbed the public address microphone and famously upbraided the team for its "stupid" play.[13]

Ironically, however, Giannoulas was first mentioned by name in the newspapers as a frog. Still working for KGB's promotions department in August 1974, he set the world record for go-kart driving at the El Cajon Carting Center while dressed as Tyrone the Frog.[14]

He continued to appear at San Diego Stadium throughout 1975, and by 1976 other teams had taken notice of the Chicken's antics. Giannoulas was invited by St. Louis Cardinals trainer Gene Gieselmann to Busch Stadium in August 1976.[15] There, he armwrestled Keith Hernandez, got an autographed bat from Red Schoendienst and entertained the fans, all while unabashedly rooting for the visiting Padres.[16] Capping off his successful year, Giannoulas was awarded the 1976 Sports Performance MVP by the *San Diego Evening Tribune*, beating out Padres Cy Young

Award-winner Randy Jones and Chargers receiver Charlie Joyner.[17]

Commissioner Bowie Kuhn was scheduled to be in San Diego for the 1977 home opener and called the Padres with an offer to throw out the ceremonial first ball of the season.[18] Kuhn was rebuffed—the Padres had already promised the honor to the Chicken.[19] After practicing all day at Hoover High School's baseball field, Giannoulas took the mound on April 12 and threw a strike, but not before he used the rosin bag as a deodorant and groomed the mound on all fours, just like Mark "The Bird" Fidrych. On May 28, the Chicken got to perform on the field for the first time while participating in a commercial shoot during the fifth-inning break. With no real plan, Giannoulas decided to wing it. He pantomimed spectacular plays at shortstop and engaged umpire Art Williams—much to his surprise—all to howling approval.[20]

Padres executive Ballard Smith told Giannoulas that Atlanta Braves owner Ted Turner proposed a trade at the 1978 owners meetings that would have sent the Padres a backup catcher in exchange for the Chicken. After he was advised the Chicken was not the Padres' asset to trade—Giannoulas was still employed by KGB—Turner set out to lure him to Atlanta. While Giannoulas was appearing for a game at Fulton County Stadium in early September 1978, Turner offered him $50,000 (not chicken feed; this is about $191,000 today) to move to Atlanta and give life to a new character. When Giannoulas—who still lived at home—was hesitant, Turner increased the offer to $100,000, threw in a television show, and promised an office next to Hank Aaron![21] After an outpouring of pleas from San Diegans, including Mayor Pete Wilson, Giannoulas ultimately decided to stay in San Diego.[22] For his loyalty, KGB agreed to pay Giannoulas $50,000 per year, making him the second-highest paid employee at the station and equaling the yearly salary of Padres hurler Bob Shirley.[23] Giannoulas was also granted permission to accept payment for out-of-town appearances as the KGB Chicken.[24]

During his reign as the KGB Chicken, KGB's ratings climbed from fifth in San Diego to first, Giannoulas won an Emmy for a KGB commercial, and he was awarded a commendation from the state legislature for his "comedy contributions to the State of California." When a regional magazine polled Padres fans, 11 percent said they came to the games just to see the Chicken.[25] At the time, Tony Gwynn was a two-sport star at San Diego State. He often went to Padres games "and a lot of times it was to see the Chicken. I loved [Dave] Winfield and Ozzie [Smith] at the end, but you know after a while, it was 'Hey, the Chicken—what's the Chicken doing?'"[26]

CRACKS APPEAR

When Giannoulas performed in Seattle on May 4, 1979, for a nationally televised NBA playoff game, he did so without displaying the KGB logo, which ruffled the feathers of KGB management. Giannoulas was fired and made the defendant in a $250,000 breach of contract lawsuit filed by KGB.[27] At a May 23 hearing, Giannoulas was stripped of the chicken suit and barred from appearing in the costume in San Diego and the surrounding counties.[28]

Giannoulas, however, was ready for a fight. With the help of his mother and sister, Giannoulas designed a new chicken costume, complete with his very own logo.[29] He struck a deal with the Padres and held a press conference at the ball park on June 25 from inside the giant Styrofoam egg, forcing reporters to put their ears and microphones up to the shell. Giannoulas invited all to witness the "Grand Hatching" ceremony planned for the June 29 game against the visiting Astros.[30]

Throughout that week, the giant egg was on display in the right-field pavilion—only to disappear the night before the Grand Hatching was set to take place. Although KGB was an immediate suspect, the station was cleared once the actual thieves sobered up and contacted the local news to broker a deal for the return of the egg. Their demands included that no charges be filed and that they be given twelve tickets to the Grand Hatching game and all the beer they could drink; Giannoulas had little choice but talked them down to four tickets and $20 for beer.[31]

Prior to the start of that June 29 game, the capacity crowd chanted, "We want the chicken!" as the outfield gates opened and the egg—perched precariously atop an armored truck and with a California Highway Patrol motorcycle escort—made its way to

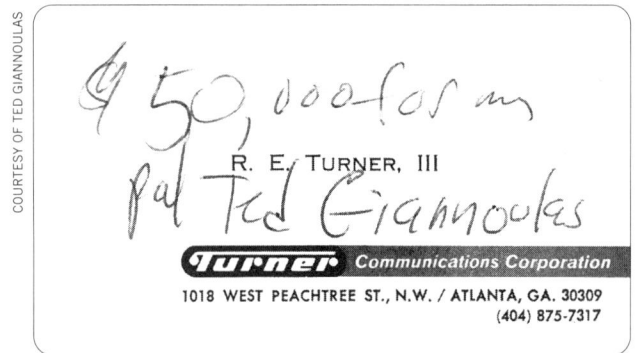

R. E. TURNER, III

Turner Communications Corporation
1018 WEST PEACHTREE ST., N.W. / ATLANTA, GA. 30309
(404) 875-7317

Atlanta Braves owner Ted Turner memorialized his initial employment offer to Ted Giannoulas on his business card.

third base.[32] After being placed gently on the ground, the egg began to roll around and came to rest as Giannoulas burst triumphantly from the shell, revealing the San Diego Chicken to the world.[33] Shrewdly, Giannoulas had negotiated a deal with the Padres in which he would be compensated a portion of each ticket sold above average attendance, pocketing in excess of $40,000 for the Grand Hatching spectacle. That money was applied directly to his mounting legal fees, as he continued to fight the lawsuit filed by KGB and separate contempt charges KGB brought against Giannoulas for continuing to make appearances.[34]

CHICKEN SUITS

In 1980, Giannoulas scored a pair of significant legal victories. On April 16, the San Diego Superior Court dismissed the contempt charges brought by KGB following a two-day hearing that culminated in the San Diego Chicken and KGB Chicken standing side-by-side in the courtroom. Judge Raul Rosario held that the costumes were not "substantially similar," which made Giannoulas a "free bird."[35]

Shortly thereafter, the appeal of KGB's suit for breach of his employment contract was decided in favor of Giannoulas.[36] Justice Gerald Brown proclaimed, "Silly though the issues appear at first glance, the underlying principles are serious."[37] The reviewing court held that Giannoulas's post-employment performances in a chicken costume were neither competitive nor unfair because he did not sport the station logo or otherwise imply that he represented KGB radio.[38] Further, the chicken costume designed by Giannoulas and his family was not "substantially similar" and the court could not ban him from appearing in "any chicken suit whatsoever."[39] The injunction entered by the lower court prohibiting him from performing in a chicken suit in San Diego and adjacent counties had improperly restricted Giannoulas's "rights to earn a living and to express himself as an artist."[40]

Relying on a precedential case involving Bela Lugosi's movie portrayal of Dracula, the court found, "masked or not, both Lugosi and Giannoulas have made certain roles their own, by a combination of mannerisms, gestures, body language, and other behavior adding up in each case to a unique character."[41] The court also found unpersuasive KGB's claim that it made no difference who wore the costume, "if that were so, why did KGB pay Giannoulas some $50,000 a year to wear it?"[42] Ultimately, the court found in favor of Giannoulas on all counts, except that he was prohibited from making any further appearances as the KGB Chicken.[43]

FREE BIRD

Once free of the KGB litigation, Giannoulas was truly able to spread his wings, making upwards of 250 appearances per year all over the country, and eventually the world. By his count, Giannoulas has performed live in front of millions of fans at over 8,500 games.

He starred on *The Baseball Bunch*, a television program hosted by Johnny Bench.[44] Bench knew Giannoulas well from the Big Red Machine days, when the two often conspired to pull pranks on Pete Rose.[45] In fact, Bench has warmly referred to the Chicken as his "idol."[46] Giannoulas's favorite memory of The Baseball Bunch was when Ted Williams appeared on the show to do some hitting demonstrations, bringing together Hoover High School's most famous graduates. On the big screen, the Chicken had a cameo role in the cult classic *Attack of the Killer Tomatoes*.[47]

But the Chicken's shtick is not for everyone. Lou Piniella once threw his glove at the Chicken after he put a "hex" on Yankees pitcher Ron Guidry during a game against Seattle at the Kingdome in 1979.[48] "We win the pennant, and they want to make the Chicken bigger than the team," groused Padres general manager Jack McKeon after the Padres qualified for the 1984 World Series. "Marketing people thought he was the reason we were putting people in the ballpark. ... Do your act and get the hell off of the field."[49]

The San Diego Chicken flies safely into third base.

Giannoulas has also had to defend himself in court on several other occasions. Pitcher Don Schulze sued him for $2 million, claiming the Chicken separated his shoulder during an exhibition game in 1981 when Schulze was a member of the Quad Cities Cubs.[50] Giannoulas was exonerated after the jury watched a video of the incident.[51] Giannoulas also prevailed in a lawsuit brought by the intellectual property owners of the Barney character in 1999. They were offended by a skit in which the Chicken would "flip, slap, tackle, trample, and generally assault" a Barney look-alike called "Duffy the Dragon."[52] The court held that the performance was a parody and "denying parodists the opportunity to poke fun at symbols and names which have become woven into the fabric of our daily life would constitute a serious curtailment of a protected form of expression."[53] More recently, Giannoulas successfully fended off a lawsuit filed by a fan hit by a foul ball at a 2004 Dayton Dragons game who claimed she was distracted by the Chicken.[54]

FEATHERS IN HIS CAP

Proving that good things come in small peck-ages, the San Diego Chicken remains an innovative and enduring figure in sports entertainment. Giannoulas was the first mascot to talk and make noises as part of his act and, through his routines, introduced pre-recorded music to the ballpark.[55] He broke new ground with his own card in the 1982 Donruss baseball set—the first fan to be featured in a nationally distributed issue.[56] He was named one of the 100 Most Powerful Sports Figures of the 20th Century by *The Sporting News*, right behind Wayne Gretzky.[57] The Chicken was even honored with his own bobblehead night at Qualcomm Stadium on September 26, 2003.[58]

Giannoulas was an inaugural inductee into the Mascot Hall of Fame in 2005 and was inducted into The Baseball Reliquary's Shrine of Eternals on July 16, 2011.[59] His San Diego Chicken costume is featured prominently at the National Baseball Museum in Cooperstown and another Chicken head is displayed at the Gerald Ford Presidential Museum in Grand Rapids, Michigan.[60] In 2018, an authenticated Chicken head sold for nearly $10,000 at auction.[61]

Giannoulas is "semiretired" now but plans to perform as long as he is physically able, including appearances with the Padres in 2019 to help commemorate the team's 50th anniversary.[62] And perhaps the man in the chicken suit said it best: "There's no way, really, of knowing what the future holds, but I hope there are many more laughs ahead for us."[63] ∎

Notes

1. "Chicken Man Hatched Again," *Austin American-Statesman*, June 30, 1979.
2. *The Los Angeles Times*, June 30, 1979.
3. Ted Giannoulas, telephone interview, January 14, 2019.
4. Giannoulas is known as the San Diego Chicken, the Famous Chicken and the Famous San Diego Chicken. He uses these interchangeably, depending on whether he is performing somewhere fans might not take kindly to a visiting or rival mascot.
5. Giannoulas, telephone interview. He fondly recalled listening to Harry Caray with the Cardinals, Bob Prince with the Pirates, Lindsay Nelson with the Mets, and Joe Nuxhall with the Cincinnati Reds.
6. "The Giants' fowl friend," King Thompson, *San Francisco Examiner*, April 22, 1982.
7. Giannoulas, telephone interview.
8. Giannoulas.
9. Ron Hutcherson, "The Chick Col. Sanders Forgot," *Press Democrat* (Santa Rosa, CA), July 31, 1977.
10. Ted Giannoulas, telephone interview, January 14, 2019.
11. Giannoulas.
12. KGB Chicken (Ted Giannoulas), *From Scratch* (San Diego: Joyce Press, 1978), 7.
13. Phil Collier, "Padre Kroc Eats Humble Pie After 'Stupid' Slur," *The Sporting News*, April 27, 1974.
14. "Young Women Set Nonstop Go-Cart Mark," *Progress Bulletin* (Pomona, CA), August 21, 1974. (Giannoulas drove for 75 hours and 26 minutes.)
15. KGB Chicken, From *Scratch*, 61.
16. *From Scratch*.
17. "Chicken-Man MVP," *Chicago Tribune*, January 1, 1977.
18. Mike Lopresti, "In San Diego, the 'Chicken Game' is Baseball," *Palladium-Item* (Richmond, IN), July 16, 1978.
19. Lopresti.
20. KGB Chicken, *From Scratch*, 42–3, 46–7.
21. Giannoulas, telephone interview. Giannoulas had also separately been offered a three-year, $225,000 pact by KVI and the Seattle Mariners.
22. "$100,000 Chicken Feed to Ted Turner," *Atlanta Constitution*, September 14, 1978. (California Governor Pete Wilson later hosted "Chicken Day" and honored Giannoulas for taking "a Sherman-like stand on an attempted coup bordering on chicken-snatching on the part of Atlanta.") "'Hysterical Landmark' Becoming Free Agent?" *Tampa Tribune*, May 11, 1979.
23. Giannoulas, telephone interview; "Bob Shirley," Baseball Reference, https://www.baseball-reference.com/players/s/shirlbo01.shtml.
24. "$50,000 Chicken is Fired," *Press Democrat*, May 9, 1979.
25. Patricia Lee Murphy, "Looking for Some Chicken Delight? Just Order Up Ted Giannoulas, Who's Sure Not to Lay An Egg," *People*, September 25, 1978.
26. "Chicken Bids Goodbye to Where it All Began," *The New York Times*, September 28, 2003.
27. "$50,000 Chicken is Fired."
28. "Mascot is Stripped of Chicken Suit," *Minneapolis Star*, May 30, 1979.
29. "He'll Still Roost with San Diego Team," *Lansing* (Michigan) *State Journal*, June 24, 1979. (If you look closely at the Chicken's logo, you will see that the middle of the "C" is cleverly shaped like an egg.)
30. "'The Chicken' Plots Return," *Tulare* (California) *Advance-Register*, June 26, 1979.
31. Giannoulas, telephone interview; Steve Dolan, "Giannoulas Can't Egg the Astros Into a Defeat, 4–1," *Los Angeles* Times, 1:III.
32. "It's a Bird/The Chicken Re-hatches," *San Bernardino County Sun*, June 30, 1979.
33. The Famous Chicken, "The Grand Hatching" video, YouTube, https://www.youtube.com/watch?v=IVrDjDyHJwY=.
34. Giannoulas, telephone interview. "'I'm a Free Bird,' Giannoulas 35 Crows," *Los Angeles Times*, April 17, 1980.
36. *KGB, Inc. v. Giannoulas*, 104 Cal.App.3d 844 (1980).

37. *KGB, Inc. v. Giannoulas* at 846.
38. *KGB, Inc. v. Giannoulas* at 850.
39. *KGB, Inc. v. Giannoulas* at 847. (The injunction had forbidden Giannoulas from appearing anywhere in the KGB Chicken costume or any "substantially similar" costume; in any "chicken ensemble or suit whatsoever" in San Diego County or an adjacent county; and, in a chicken suit at any sports or public event in which a team from San Diego County appears.)
40. *KGB, Inc. v. Giannoulas.*
41. *KGB, Inc. v. Giannoulas* at 855.
42. *KGB, Inc. v. Giannoulas.*
43. *KGB, Inc. v. Giannoulas* at 853.
44. Giannoulas, telephone interview.
45. Bill Francis, "San Diego Chicken Lands at Doubleday Field," *Freeman's Journal*, July 30, 1999.
46. Dan Barriero, "Ted Giannoulas Winds Up Making More Than Just Chicken Feed," *Los Angeles Times*, August 27, 1983.
47. Giannoulas, telephone interview.
48. "Mariners 5, Yankees 1" *Herald-Palladium* (St. Joseph, MI), July 11, 1979.
49. "Mickey Mouse, Ronald McDonald don't make cut," ESPN.com, August 16, 2005. http://www.espn.com/espn/news/story?id=2135976.
50. Mandy Mueller, "Pitcher Says 'Chicken' Tackled Him," UPI, October 16, 1985. https://www.upi.com/Archives/1985/10/16/Pitcher-says-Chicken-tackled-him/5712498283200/.
51. Mueller; *Schulze v. Chicken's Co.*, 802 F.2d 464 (Table) (8th Cir., 1986).
52. *Lyons Partnership v. Giannoulas*, 179 F.3d 384 (C.A.5 (Tex.), 1999); see also https://www.youtube.com/watch?v=5UmgRjgeRpM.
53. *Lyons Partnership v. Giannoulas*, 14 F.Supp.2d 947, 953 (N.D. Tex., 1998). *Harting v. Dayton Dragons Professional*,
54. 870 N.E.2d 766 (Ohio App., 2007). (Giannoulas did lose a personal injury case involving a Chicago Bulls cheerleader. Smyth v. Giannoulas, 1991L019113, Cook County, Illinois, May 1996.)
55. Giannoulas, telephone interview.
56. Associated Press, "Now That He's a Card, Will He Lay an Egg?," *San Francisco Examiner*, December 23, 1981.
57. "100 Most Powerful Sports Figures of the 20th Century," *The Sporting News*, December 20, 1999.
58. Associated Press, "Chicken Bids Goodbye to Where it all Began," *The New York Times*, September 28, 2003.
59. "Baseball Reliquary to hold 'Shrine of the Eternals' induction," *The Sun* (San Bernardino), July 13, 2011. (To be eligible for induction into the Mascot Hall of Fame, a mascot must have been in existence at least 10 years; have a major impact on its sport, industry and community; and have a performance that is consistently memorable and groundbreaking.)
60. Hall of Fame clipping file; Giannoulas, telephone interview.
61. LOT #852: San Diego Chicken Mascot Head, GoldinAuctions.com, https://goldinauctions.com/San_Diego_Chicken_Mascot_Head-LOT39293.aspx, accessed February 11, 2019.
62. Giannoulas, telephone interview.
63. KGB Chicken, From *Scratch*, 94.

Alan Wiggins

A Tragic Hero

Fred O. Rodgers

In early February 1985, Alan Wiggins became the newest big-money player for the 1984 National League champion San Diego Padres. With the help of his San Diego-based agent, Tony Attanasio, and Padres general manager Jack McKeon, Wiggins, just 26 years old, signed a guaranteed four-year, $2.5 million contract, making him one of the highest paid second basemen in the game.

Wiggins had been in arbitration and was seeking a one-year deal for $525,000. The Padres were offering $425,000, but in the end they agreed to $2.5 million over four years, which would be an annual average of $625,000.[1]

Was it a wise move by the Padres? Hindsight shows it was anything but. The 1984 season had been Wiggins' first at second base after shifting from left field, where he'd played the previous two seasons with the team. Padres management wanted to get rookie power hitter Carmelo Martinez into the lineup, but his usual spot was first base, which was manned by Steve Garvey. Martinez wasn't going to bump Garvey from the lineup, so he went to left field and Wiggins moved to second.

Playing the infield wasn't new to Wiggins. He had played second base when he was signed in 1978 and had even played a year of shortstop in the minor leagues. But this was the majors, and a huge experiment for the team.

Wiggins began the 1984 season with 11 errors in the first 29 games, but he relaxed a bit and made only 21 more errors the rest of the season—still not great but an improvement.

It was on offense that Wiggins proved most beneficial to the Padres during their pennant run. Leading off, he batted .258 for the year, but scored 106 runs, setting a team record, and his 70 stolen bases also eclipsed his own team mark of 66 in 1983.[2]

Wiggins's 75 walks and 154 hits helped Tony Gwynn win his first of eight National League batting titles. With Wiggins a threat on the bases, pitchers had to throw a lot of fastballs, and Gwynn was ready for them, batting .412 with Wiggins on base.[3] Gwynn's overall batting average was .351.

Moving Wiggins to second base was a gamble. Manager Dick Williams forced Padres management to release backup Juan Bonilla, the 1983 starter, so Wiggins wouldn't have to look over his shoulder.[4] Not too many managers would have released a player who had over 550 at-bats the year before and would have been insurance if the shift of Wiggins hadn't worked out.

After the season, Williams said, "Wiggins was the Most Valuable Player in the National League in 1984. Without him we don't win the pennant."[5] Padres president Ballard Smith agreed, "No player made a more outstanding contribution to our success last season than Alan Wiggins," he said. "He had a tremendous impact on our club." Smith also mentioned that Wiggins was praised for his work with the San Diego Police Department for counseling youths about drug abuse.[6]

Wiggins was now at the top of his game. He had financial security, he worked with the community, and he was roundly praised. But it was all a façade. After he signed his contract, it would be all downhill: Six years later, Alan Wiggins would be dead—the first major-league player known to have died from AIDS. While counseling kids on drug use, he had needed somebody to step in and help him.

* * *

Alan Wiggins was born on February 17, 1958, to Albert and Karla Wiggins in Pasadena, California. His parents divorced when he was only a year old. The family moved a few miles north of Pasadena to Altadena, where Alan and his older brother, Donald, were raised by their single mom.

Wiggins was always angry that he never had a dad around him to help him achieve success in life.[7] A great athlete as a youngster, he started playing in Little League in the mid-1960s. Pasadena schools didn't integrate until 1969 and its Little League teams were segregated.[8] Wiggins knew racial tension before he was a teenager.

By the time he got to high school, schools in California had initiated forced busing to integrate the schools. Wiggins was bused to John Muir High School in Pasadena, which Jackie Robinson had attended.

When a white schoolmate showed him a baseball card of Robinson, Wiggins bullied him to give up the card. Wiggins thought he deserved it more since he was black.[9] That sense of entitlement would be part of his personality for the rest of his life.

Following a couple of successful seasons of high school baseball, Wiggins went to Pasadena Community College in 1976 and played baseball, again following in the footsteps of Jackie Robinson.

Wiggins's racial consciousness increased at PCC when he read *The Autobiography of Malcolm X*. He would continue to study the life of Malcolm X, as well as Nation of Islam leader Elijah Muhammad, for years afterward.[10] The book had a profound effect on his personality—in both good and bad ways, Wiggins admitted.[11]

Baseball scouts followed Wiggins's career at PCC. The California Angels drafted him with the eighth overall pick in the regular phase of the January draft in 1977, and Wiggins signed for $2,500 in May, after the college season ended.[12]

Wiggins was sent to Idaho Falls in the Pioneer League in June 1977 to play second base. He batted .271 and stole 25 bases in 63 games. The next season he was sent to Quad Cities in the Midwest League, where his batting average dropped to .201 and he had 26 stolen bases in 49 games. A midseason fight with his manager resulted in the Angels releasing him.[13] His temper had become an issue.

Since the Dodgers had wanted to sign him when he was at PCC, Wiggins contacted the club about a tryout. He auditioned for manager Tommy Lasorda, who was impressed and signed the 20-year-old to play shortstop for the Dodgers' Class A affiliate, Clinton of the Midwest League, where he had played the year before.[14] Wiggins batted .257 in 95 games and stole 43 bases.

In 1980 Wiggins made his biggest impressions with the Dodgers, good and bad. He stole a league-record 120 bases in 135 games for Lodi in the California League. He also batted a career-best .288 with 108 runs scored. The bad was a marijuana arrest in June.[15]

As a four-year minor leaguer, he was available in the Rule 5 draft for the price of $25,000. The Dodgers didn't protect him by putting him on their 40-man roster. The team never stated his arrest was a reason for not doing so, but this was a player who had just set a league stolen-base record. Why would a team let him go?

McKeon had seen Wiggins in one game, and that was enough. The Padres drafted him. Team officials

Padres manager Dick Williams said of Alan Wiggins: "Wiggins was the Most Valuable Player in the National League in 1984. Without him we don't win the pennant."

later said that they knew of his arrest.[16] Joan Kroc, owner Ray Kroc's wife, had initiated Operation Cork in 1976 to promote awareness of chemical dependency and its impact on families. In 1980, the Padres were one of the first teams to set up an employee assistance program to help players and staff with alcohol, chemical dependence, and other problems.[17]

Wiggins was given all the printed materials the organization had on the subject of chemical dependency. Texas Rangers star Ferguson Jenkins had been arrested in Toronto in 1980 on drug charges. That was a start to baseball's worst decade for recreational drug abuse.[18]

The Padres sent Wiggins to Hawaii, their Triple-A affiliate in the Pacific Coast League, to learn to play the outfield. The club hoped his speed would allow him to cover the left field line. The good news: He batted .302 and had 73 stolen bases in 133 games. The bad news: He was arrested on marijuana charges again.[19]

The other alarming fact was that Hawaii manager Doug Rader called Wiggins into his office after a night game and the two of them argued about Wiggins's sensitivity around racial issues. According to teammates, after about 30 minutes of loud, abusive language, the two emerged with arms around each other.[20] Problem resolved.

Wiggins started the 1982 season back in Hawaii. After just 19 games, he was batting .312 with 21 stolen bases, and the Padres called him up to replace injured left fielder Gene Richards.[21]

Two months later, on July 19, the Padres' lineup was changed for the next 20 years when Gwynn was recalled. With Wiggins in left field and Gwynn in center, they seemed to have things covered for quite a while.

But just two days later—July 21, 1982—Wiggins was arrested at 2:30 AM with a gram of cocaine in his possession. Under MLB guidelines, had Wiggins come forward with a drug problem and gone to rehab, he'd have received no penalty. But since his dependency came to light when he was arrested, he was suspended for 30 days. Wiggins served his rehab at the Orange County Rehabilitation Center in Anaheim from August 20 to September 19.[22]

He came back on September 20 and finished the season batting .256 with 33 stolen bases. He only appeared in 72 games in 1982.

Wiggins had his finest year to date in 1983. He batted .276 with 66 stolen bases, setting a franchise record. He played 63 games in left (31 as a starter), 49 in center, but most of the last 45 games of the year at first base, replacing the injured Garvey. He was voted the Padres' Most Valuable Player.[23] Even better than that: There were no drug arrests or suspensions.

The only complaint heard during the year was about his attitude on race. On a team plane, Wiggins lost a card game to Kurt Bevacqua, who told him not to renege on paying off the loss. "Don't be a renegger," Bevacqua said facetiously. Wiggins took offense, thinking it was a racial epithet, and he had to be restrained.[24]

"Alan thought the whole world was racist," said Gary Hyvonen, a sportswriter for the Oceanside *Blade-Citizen* in the San Diego suburb of Oceanside. Wiggins's agent, Tony Attanasio, also weighed in. "Suffice to say," he said, "what Alan thinks was racist wasn't necessarily so."[25]

In the pennant-winning 1984 season, Wiggins was praised for having another good year, and especially for avoiding drug problems and personality conflicts. He excelled in the postseason by batting .316 against the Chicago Cubs in the NLCS and then notching eight hits and a .364 batting average in the World Series (second only to Bevacqua's .410). The Detroit Tigers won the Series in five games, but Wiggins had become a star, and his new four-year contract seemed to back up that status. He couldn't wait until spring training opened in 1985.

With his wife, Angie, expecting their third child soon, the security of the guaranteed contract took the pressure off him during spring training for the first time. It was now all about getting ready and playing up to the expectations of a major league second baseman.

With one week left in spring training, Wiggins hurt his knee, his first significant injury. He missed the last few games of the spring and the first few games of the regular season.

The Padres were putting a little bit of pressure on him to get into the games due to the big contract he had signed. Wiggins struggled on his return, batting only .054 (2-for-37) with no stolen bases in April.

Wiggins was a no-show for the opener of a four-game series against the Dodgers on Thursday night, April 25. The Padres searched for him in vain until Sunday, when the front office received a call from a rehab center in Minnesota telling them that Wiggins had checked himself in for a relapse of cocaine dependency.

Joan Kroc was outraged.

She decided that Wiggins would never play for the Padres again.[26] Since his other cocaine suspension had been in 1982, before the major league agreement on rehabilitation regulations was initiated in 1984, this was technically his first offense. But the Padres did not want to activate him after his treatment was concluded. Donald Fehr, the players association counsel, threatened legal action, so the Padres activated Wiggins and traded him to the Baltimore Orioles on July 27.

Alan Wiggins's career with the San Diego Padres was finished with less than one year completed on his four-year contract.

Wiggins struggled in Baltimore. His history of drug arrests didn't seem to suit Orioles fans, who booed him. He sometimes didn't run out ground balls and failed to make a full effort on defense. He fell into disfavor with manager Earl Weaver by 1986 and then with new manager Cal Ripken Sr. the next year. He was suspended in July 1987 for fighting with a teammate before a game.[27]

Wiggins was suspended indefinitely on September 1 after failing a drug test.[28] His baseball career was over, though he still had the income from his guaranteed contract through 1988. He continued to abuse cocaine, and he contracted HIV through his use of needles.

In November 1990, Wiggins was hospitalized at Cedars-Sinai Medical Center in Los Angeles with complications from AIDS, including pneumonia and tuberculosis. After falling in and out of consciousness for about a month, he died on January 6, 1991.[29] He was 32 years old.

Only two former teammates attended his funeral, Steve Garvey and Lee Lacy.[30]

Sidenote: Alan's wife, Angie, never told their children anything negative about their father. She only told them about the positives of his life. She steered all three kids toward basketball, away from their father's game. All three earned college basketball scholarships: Cassandra at New York University; Alan Jr. at the University of San Francisco; and Candice at Stanford.[31]

Alan Jr. had a long career playing pro basketball overseas. Candice was a four-time All-American at Stanford and then had an eight-year career in the WNBA. She has partnered with Until There's a Cure, a nonprofit organization that raises awareness and funds to combat AIDS.[32]

In 2017 she was the first female basketball player inducted into the Breitbard Hall of Fame, which honors San Diego athletes.[33] She says her career was blessed by all the good things she learned about her father. To this day, she says, her dad, Alan Wiggins, is her hero. ■

Notes

1. Phil Collier, "Wiggins Signs $2.5 Million Contract," *The Sporting News*, February 25,1985.
2. David Porter and Joe Naiman, *The San Diego Padres Encyclopedia* (Champaign, IL, Sports Publishing, 2002).
3. Victor Dighe, "The Evil I Do Not Intend," *San Diego Reader*, June 15, 1995.
4. Steve Dolan, "Wiggins Puts Padres in Winning Groove," *Baseball Gold*, July 1, 1983.
5. Dick Williams and Bill Plaschke, *No More Mr. Nice Guy*, (San Diego: Harcourt Brace Jovanovich, 1990).
6. Collier, "Wiggins Signs $2.5 Million Contract."
7. Dolan, "Wiggins Puts Padres in Winning Groove."
8. Steven Roberts, "Pasadena Adjusts to Busing, But Opposition Remains," *The New York Times* , November 21,1971.
9. Dolan, "Wiggins Puts Padres in Winning Groove."
10. Dighe, "The Evil I Do Not Intend."
11. Alan Wiggins, interview, August 19, 1984.
12. "Alan Wiggins, once called the fastest man on two feet," UPI, July 22,1982.
13. UPI.
14. UPI.
15. Porter and Naiman, *The San Diego Padres Encyclopedia.*
16. Williams and Plaschke, *No More Mr. Nice Guy.*
17. "Alan Wiggins, once called the fastest man on two feet."
18. Chronology of Baseball Drug Cases Since 1980," *Los Angeles Times*, May 12, 1985.
19. Alan Wiggins, interview.
20. Tony Gwynn, interview with Fred O. Rodgers, August 19, 1984.
21. Porter and Naiman, *The San Diego Padres Encyclopedia.*
22. Hilmer Anderson, "Wiggins 'Truly Sorry,'" UPI, August 27, 1982.
23. "Alan Wiggins, once called the fastest man on two feet."
24. Kurt Bevacqua, interview with Fred O. Rodgers, January 19, 2019.
25. Dighe, "The Evil I Do Not Intend."
26. Phil Collier, "Wiggins Out For Year For Drug Treatment," *The Sporting News*, May 13, 1985.
27. Kent Baker, "Wiggins recalled as an angry talent," *Baltimore Sun*, January 9, 1991, https://www.baltimoresun.com/news/bs-xpm-1991-01-09-1991009005-story.html.
28. Dighe, "The Evil I Do Not Intend."
29. Dighe.
30. Dighe.
31. Candice Wiggins as told to Whitney Joiner, "How Candice Wiggins Overcame the 'Shame' of Her Father's Death," espnW, September 28, 2015.
32. "Candice Wiggins: Phenom With A Cause," Until.org, https://web.archive.org/web/20100613112725/http://until.org/news/2009/candice_wiggins.shtml.
33. Tod Leonard, "Entering Hall, Wiggins Finds Peace in Father's Legacy," *San Diego Union-Tribune*, February 20, 2017.

Rupe's Troops, No Más Monge, and Tempy Turns It Around

Part of the Padres Golden Era

Brian P. Wood

The San Diego Padres had a miserable start to their existence. In their first 13 seasons, only once did they finish above .500, in 1978, with a record of 84–78. The second time they would accomplish this feat, their reward would be the 1984 World Series. It was part of the Padres first Golden Era, 1982–85, when they would run off four consecutive .500-plus campaigns and from May 1984 to May 1985 were the best team in the National League West.

These are stories of three key ingredients in transforming the Padres from an also-ran to an elite major-league team.

1982: RUPE'S TROOPS

"Rooooop! Rooooop!" In the long tradition of major leaguers with an "*oo*" sound in their names (from B-*oo*-g-Powell to M-*oo*-kie Betts) came Ruppert (R-*oo*-pert) Jones.

Jones attended high school in Berkeley, California, playing in the same outfield with future big-leaguers Claudell Washington and Glenn Burke.[1] Taken from the Kansas City Royals by the Seattle Mariners with the first pick in the 1976 expansion draft, Jones gained immediate popularity in the Emerald City with his spectacular play in center field.[2] The adoring fans came to be known as "Roop's Troops." He was an All-Star in 1977, while in 1979 he set career highs in runs (109), hits (166), triples (9), RBIs (78), and stolen bases (33).

Ruppert Jones played for the San Diego Padres from 1981–83. After his hot start in 1982, his fans became known as Rupe's Troops supporting him in throngs in the center-field bleachers.

Jones ended up in San Diego in 1981, where he would anchor the Padres outfield for three seasons. After a horrific start, batting .185 in mid-May, Jones went on an 18-for-49 tear (.367), giving Padres fans a look at his potential. He finished the year at .250.

He started 1982 firing on all cylinders and was batting .356 on June 1. This, along with a team-record 11-game win streak in April, reignited the Rupe's Troops craze (with the new spelling), with fans and teammates proudly wearing T-shirts bearing the slogan.[3] At the end of warm-up tosses prior to each inning, Jones would throw the ball into the center-field stands (a practice that was not as commonplace as it is today), further endearing him to the fans. Coach Bobby Tolan remarked, "When it comes to working hard, Tim Flannery and Ruppert are numbers one and two."[4]

He was selected as the Padres' lone representative in the 1982 All-Star Game, where he knocked a pinch-hit triple off Dennis Eckersley of the Boston Red Sox.

Two weeks later, Jones twisted his ankle and heel, causing him to miss nearly a month of the season.[5] After returning, he was unable to regain his prior level of excellence. At the time of the injury, he had a slash line of .303/.399/.467. For the remainder of the season, he fell to .218/.286/.287 with no home runs.

His hitting woes would continue into 1983 (.233, 12 HR, 49 RBIs). His power would undergo a resurgence, but not with the Padres. He signed as a free agent with the Detroit Tigers where he slugged .516 and played on their 1984 World Series team against the Padres. He signed with the California Angels in 1985 and slugged .447 with 21 home runs.

Jones's presence on the Padres added a stabilizing influence on a team that was trying to create a winning atmosphere.

1983: "NO MÁS MONGE," THE RISE AND FALL OF A PADRES RELIEVER

Isidro "Sid" Monge, born in Mexico and raised in California, hit his stride with the Cleveland Indians in the late 1970s, earning an All-Star slot in 1979 as he sported career bests in saves (19), ERA (2.40), and

Sid Monge, reliever for the San Diego Padres. He started his tenure with 15⅓ scoreless innings in 1983, but lost his control the next season and was dispatched to the Tigers in June.

WAR (5.6). He was awarded Cleveland's 1979 Good Guy Award, given to a player for his cooperation with the public and media.[6] "Even during tough times, I have always had time to talk," Monge said.[7] But his performance dipped in 1981 and he was dispatched to Philadelphia.

The Padres were hungry to bolster their bullpen and in May 1983 they acquired the veteran lefty from the Phillies. Monge had previously established a good relationship with both manager Dick Williams and pitching coach Norm Sherry, having played for both in the Angels organization in the early 1970s. Monge felt that both understood his need to be used frequently and in tight situations. "Sid is primarily a power pitcher, who also has a good slow curve," Williams said upon Monge's arrival on the West Coast.[8]

His start with the Padres was spectacular: He gave up no runs in his first 15.1 innings over 10 outings. His superb mound work continued over his next 21 outings (2.83 ERA) before he went into a short slump (14 runs allowed in 14 innings). That began on August 26 after a hard comebacker up the middle by Andre Dawson of the Chicago Cubs hit Monge in the head.[9] He closed the season with a flurry, allowing just one run in his last 10-plus innings. Monge racked up seven saves and seven wins for the Pads with an ERA of 3.15 (ERA+ 113). "It makes a difference when you get to pitch when the game means something," he said.[10] The Padres ended with an 81–81 record for the second consecutive year.

Going into 1984, San Diego was picked to finish first in the National League West by the Gannett News Service and second by the Associated Press.[11] Analysis provided by Bill James in his 1984 *Baseball Abstract* predicted, "The Padres are going to be one of the most exciting teams to watch in 1984. ... They could be tough to beat."[12]

Fireman Rich "Goose" Gossage had been picked up from the New York Yankees to anchor the bullpen, while Monge was expected to be the left-handed set-up man and occasional closer. San Diego got off to a great start, winning eight of nine.

The same could not be said for Monge. Seeing his first action in the third game of the season, he entered with no outs and a runner on first in the top of the ninth, the Padres leading the Cubs, 2–1. He quickly retired the first two batters before giving up a double and an intentional walk to load the bases. Monge was not able to find the strike zone and walked Richie Hebner, plating the tying run. All was forgiven when San Diego's Champ Summers banged an RBI double to win it, 3–2. Monge got the win, not the save, and the Padres were off to a 3–0 start.

His next outing came two days later, also against Chicago, with the score knotted at three with one out and the bases loaded in the ninth inning. Chicago manager Jim Frey sent up pinch-hitter Keith Moreland. Once again, Monge could not find the plate and walked Moreland on four pitches, then Ron Cey on five to bring in two runs.[13] Williams pulled Monge as the Padres faithful voiced their displeasure.[14] After the game, Monge said, "I was all wound up and needed a strikeout. Consequently, I overthrew and couldn't get the ball over the plate."[15] The Padres again showed their mettle, answering with two runs of their own in the bottom of the ninth to send the game into extra innings. Chicago put three across in the 10th to win the game and hand the Friars their first loss in five games. In two games, Monge had given up four walks in one inning pitched and allowed three inherited runners to score.

It would be six days before Monge would be used again, this time in a mop-up role. The next day, he was brought in as a long reliever in the third in a 3–3 game against the Atlanta Braves. He pitched three innings and allowed just one unearned run (on base via a walk, however). The Padres scored three times in the bottom of the third as they defeated Atlanta, 6–4. Monge got his second win and San Diego climbed to 9–2, good for first place in the NL West by 3½ games over the Los Angeles Dodgers.

Monge appeared in three games, all losses, in a four-game series in Los Angeles, giving up five runs in four innings pitched, walking two, and allowing an inherited runner to score. The Dodgers pulled to within a game and a half of the Padres.

On May 4, Monge faced his nemesis, the Cubs, at Wrigley Field. With the game tied in the bottom of the ninth, a walk, error, sacrifice, and intentional walk loaded the bases and put the winning run on third. Once again, Frey used Moreland, who walked to force in the winning run. "He didn't throw any of the pitches close," Moreland said. "That one that was a called strike wasn't even close." Monge tried to make the best of it with some forced humor: "Anybody have any tips? I've never had anything like this happen to me before. I don't have any sense of where the plate is. This is no fun at all. This team is battling back time and again, which is the sign of an excellent ball club. I just want to be able to contribute."[16]

It was not just Monge. The entire Padres pitching staff was walking too many batters. Steve Dolan of the *Los Angeles Times* surmised, "Manager Dick Williams is on the verge of giving one of them [relievers] his walking papers. Right now, Sid Monge looms as the likely candidate."[17] Fred Mitchell of the *Chicago Tribune* called Monge "Mr. Wild-High-and-Wide."[18]

Monge's next appearance was nine days later at home against the Phillies, and again, walks did him in. In one-plus innings of work, he allowed three hits, two walks, and three runs. His next three outings appeared to be better, with no runs allowed. But digging deeper shows otherwise. Monge walked three and allowed two inherited runners to score. Williams obviously had lost confidence in the southpaw. He had gaps of 15 and six days between his next appearances and was used only in long and middle relief.

On June 10, Monge was sold to the Tigers, joining former Padres teammate Jones. Monge became just the third player to have played for both World Series teams in the same season.[19]

The Padres maintained their pace in 1984 and finished 12 games ahead of the second-place Braves to advance to the postseason for the first time in club history.

Monge was gone but not forgotten by Padres fans. San Diego's Old Mission Bay Athletic Club sponsors an annual July softball "Over-the-Line" tournament. The event features three-person softball teams playing in sand courts. Sun, beer, and competition are all part of the package, as are inventive team names. One such name gave a shoutout to both boxer Roberto Duran's most famous utterance and to Monge with the moniker "No Más Monge!"[20]

Although his 1984 season was a personal disappointment, his efforts in 1983 helped San Diego to a .500 season and his presence added to the culture of winning being established by the Padres, culminating in their advance to the World Series.

Garry Templeton seemingly changed the course of the 1984 NCLS in game three—an elimination game—with his pre-game enthusiasm, defensive plays, and bat.

1984: TEMPY TURNS IT AROUND

In December 1981, Padres general manager "Trader Jack" McKeon pulled off his second blockbuster trade with the St. Louis Cardinals in the space of a year. The first had been a 10-player deal that ended up with the Padres acquiring future catcher Terry Kennedy for Hall of Fame reliever Rollie Fingers and catcher Gene Tenace. McKeon dealt another future Hall of Famer, shortstop Ozzie Smith, and pitchers Steve Mura and Al Olmstead for outfielder Sixto Lezcano, reliever Luis DeLeon, and "troubled" shortstop Garry Templeton, the first switch-hitter to amass 100 hits from both sides of the plate in one season. The following year, the Cardinals won the World Series with the help of these two trades. In his 15 seasons in St. Louis, Smith would establish himself as an offensive threat in addition to his magical glove. However, Kennedy, Lezcano, DeLeon, and Templeton all contributed to the success of the 1982–85 Padres.[21]

With a lifetime .305 batting average coming to San Diego, Templeton would bat a mediocre .255 over his first three seasons with the Padres. Smith had a lower batting average (.249) but his glove led him to three consecutive All-Star Games and Gold Gloves (8.3 dWar over those three seasons vs. 3.0 for Templeton). During that time frame, many fans felt as though the Padres had gotten the raw end of the deal.

The end of the 1984 season found the Padres atop the NL West and facing the Cubs for the right to go to the World Series. It was not until Game Three of the League Championship Series that Templeton's stock, like the Grinch's heart, "grew three sizes that day."[22] Down two games to none by a combined score of 17–2, the Padres faced elimination in the best-of-five series. Before a record crowd of 58,346 abuzz with excitement at Jack Murphy Stadium, the Padres played in their first-ever home postseason game.

"The teams were introduced, and Templeton heard his name being called over the loudspeaker system as the shortstop and No. 8 batter in a nine-man lineup," wrote Joseph Durso in *The New York Times*. "He ran onto the field, slapped hands with his teammates, then turned to the crowd, waved his cap and raised his fist in a gesture of defiance at the Cubs and the odds."[23]

Tempy's gyrations became more pronounced as the crowd grew louder and louder. "It surprised all of us," said manager Williams, "I've never seen him so emotional. Normally, he doesn't talk much. He's no pop-off or rah-rah guy. But, if I'm walking through a jungle, he's the one I want by my side."[24]

"I was trying to get the fans to rally behind us," Templeton said. "But most of all I wanted to get my teammates going. I saw our guys just standing there, and I thought I'd do a little something to fire them up and get the adrenaline flowing. Somebody's got to do it. It worked for the Cubs with the reaction of their fans, and it can work for us here."[25]

Templeton's presence was felt from the get-go as he ended a Chicago threat in the first by making a spectacular leaping catch and roll on a Leon Durham line drive with a runner on second and two outs.[26] In the second, the Cubs got on the scoreboard after a Moreland double (not a walk!) and a Cey single. Templeton stopped the rally with a diving two-out catch of Bob Dernier's shot toward left field.[27]

Still trailing 1–0 in the bottom of the fifth, the Padres led off with singles by Kennedy and Kevin McReynolds. Up stepped Templeton. The crowd gave him a huge ovation (as they had in the third when he flied out to left field). This time he responded with a double to the left-center-field gap, knocking in two runs. He scored on an Alan Wiggins single to give the Padres a 3–1 lead.[28] Behind the five-hit pitching of Ed Whitson and Gossage, San Diego prevailed, 7–1.

After the game, Gossage said, "It was the loudest crowd I've ever heard anywhere," a significant declaration from someone who had played in two World Series in Yankee Stadium (1978 and '81).[29]

The New York Times wrote, "People were saying today that Templeton had made the key hit and the key defensive plays that helped the Padres win their first game of the National League playoff Thursday evening. And even the Cubs were conceding that the 28-year-old shortstop had fired his teammates and their fans into a frenzy that had enlivened and prolonged the playoff."[30]

San Diego would win the next two games and advance to the World Series. Steve Garvey ended Game Four with a walk-off home run in the ninth to give the Padres a 7–5 victory. Templeton singled and scored the first run of the game. In the clincher, San Diego overcame a 3–0 deficit with two runs in the sixth and four in the seventh for a 6–3 win, with Templeton adding a single to the effort. In the Fall Classic, their first, the Padres would go down quickly to the Tigers, losing 4–1.

The 1984 postseason was the highlight of Templeton's time with the Padres. He batted .333 with a .412 on-base average in the NLCS and he batted .316 in the World Series. McKeon called him the catalyst of the team, saying that defensively, "He turned everything he touched into an out."[31]

Templeton was a Silver Slugger Award winner in 1984 and an All-Star in 1985. From 1987 to '91 he carried the title of captain, a testament to the respect of his coaches and teammates. In 2015, the Padres enshrined him in their Hall of Fame.[32]

EPILOGUE

The Padres peaked early in 1985 with a 25–15 record on May 26. But they would finish the season at 83–79, good enough for their fourth consecutive record above .500. It took 15 seasons for the Padres to reach the postseason for the first time. It would take another 12 to do it again, losing the NLDS in 1996, and then making it to the World Series in 1998, where they were swept by the Yankees. Williams, still the only Padres manager never to have a losing year, was let go before the 1986 season and would go on to manage the Seattle Mariners for parts of three seasons. GM McKeon continued with the Padres through 1990, acting as field manager for the final three years. In 2003, he became the oldest manager to win the World Series, with the Florida Marlins.

With four consecutive .500 or better seasons highlighted by a trip to the World Series, 1982–85 was truly the Padres' first Golden Era, with personalities to go along with it. The shouts of "Roop, Roop," the ups and downs of Sid Monge on the mound, and Garry Templeton turning the tide for the Padres were major parts of that gilded age. ■

Notes
Baseball-Reference and Retrosheet are sources not listed in the endnotes.

1. Adam Ulrey, "Ruppert Jones," SABR Bio-Project. https://sabr.org/bioproj/person/12b9ab8b.
2. Ulrey.
3. Steve Dolan, "Swing Era Returns for Padres' Ruppert Jones," *Los Angeles Times*, July 29, 1983.
4. Dave Distel, "Padres' Decision Not to Deal Jones Has Paid Off," *Los Angeles Times*, June 4, 1982.
5. Dolan, "Swing Era Returns."
6. Chris Cobbs, "Padres Cannot Play, Deal With Phillies Anyway," *Los Angeles Times*, May 23, 1983.
7. Dolan, "Sid Monge," *Los Angeles Times*, March 13, 1984.

8. Cobbs, "Padres Cannot Play."

9. "Montefusco Sent to Yankees While Padres Lose Again," *Los Angeles Times*, August 27, 1983.

10. Dolan, "Dravecky, McReynolds Team Up, 5–3," *Los Angeles Times*, June 9, 1983.

11. "National League West Predictions," *Green Bay Press-Gazette*, March 29, 1984.

12. Bill James, *The Bill James Baseball Abstract 1984* (New York: Ballantine Books, 1984), 79 (thanks to Scott Merzbach).

13. Dolan, "First Loss," *Los Angeles Times*, April 9, 1984.

14. Fred Mitchell, "Cubs Roll," *Chicago Tribune*, April 9, 1984.

15. Dolan, "First Loss."

16. Dolan, "Chicago Strolls Past the Padres, 7–6," *Los Angeles Times*, May 5, 1984.

17. Dolan, "Chicago Strolls."

18. Mitchell, "Cubs Roll."

19. Others: The others were Jack Kramer with the Yankees and Giants in 1951 and Johnny Schmitz with the Yankees and Dodgers in 1952. Five additional players have since achieved this feat: Lonnie Smith (Cardinals-Royals, 1985), Jim Bruske (Yankees-Padres, 1998), Chris Ray (Rangers-Giants, 2010), Bengie Molina (Giants-Rangers, 2010), and Arthur Rhodes (Rangers-Cardinals, 2011). Bruske and Ray didn't apear in the World Series. In addition, in 1901, Jimmy Burke played for both the AL and NL champions, the White Sox and Pirates.

20. "No más" were the words attributed to Duran during his 1980 bout against Sugar Ray Leonard. Whether the words were a figment of announcer Howard Cosell's imagination or Duran actually said "no sigo" ("I'm not going further")," "no más" became part of the boxing and sports lexicon. Ray Monell, "Roberto Duran tells the real story behind the 'No mas' bout," *New York Daily News*, August 25, 2016. https://www.nydailynews.com/latino/roberto-duran-tells-real-story-behind-no-mas-bou-article-1.2765921.

21. A number of Templeton's actions had set off some Cardinals fans: He turned down an All-Star Game invitation in 1979 (where he would have played with Sid Monge) because he was not the starter; his fluid movement in the field caused some to label him a slacker; he had various contract disputes; and in late August 1981 he failed to run to first following a strikeout on a ball that bounced away from the catcher (he had a bad knee at the time). Templeton responded to the St. Louis boo birds with an obscene gesture, which was followed by increased booing and a second gesture. Manager Whitey Herzog called him in from the field and the two had to be pulled apart. Templeton would spend two weeks in a hospital due to depression prior to the trade to San Diego. The 10 years he played in San Diego were without controversy. Jeff Sanders, "A Padre for a decade, Garry Templeton made a home in San Diego," *San Diego Union-Tribune*, January 30, 2018. https://www.sandiegouniontribune.com/sports/padres/sd-sp-padres-garry-templeton-made-a-home-insan-diego-20180130-story.html; Joseph Durso, "Templeton Spurs on Padres," *The New York Times*, October 6, 1984. https://www.nytimes.com/1984/10/06/sports/templeton-spurs-on-padres.html.

22. Dr. Seuss, *How the Grinch Stole Christmas!* (New York: Random House, 1957).

23. Durso, "Templeton Spurs on Padres."

24. Durso, "Templeton Spurs on Padres."

25. Durso, "Templeton Spurs on Padres."

26. Durso, "Templeton Spurs on Padres."

27. Bob Kravitz, "Templeton's bat, glove ignite Padres' fire," *San Diego Union*, October 5, 1984.

28. Durso, "Templeton Spurs on Padres."

29. Jay Johnson & Joe Hughes, "Full house beats 9 Cubs," *Chicago Evening Tribune*, October 5, 1984.

30. Durso, "Templeton Spurs on Padres."

31. Bill Center, "Templeton Was 'Catalyst' of Padres' 1984 N.L. Champions," FriarWire, March 17, 2017. https://padres.mlblogs.com/templeton-was-catalyst-of-padres-1984-n-l-champions-1653906dfcf8.

32. Center, "Templeton Was Catalyst."

Steve Garvey and the Most Iconic Moment in San Diego Sports History

Kevin Mills

The San Diego Padres have retired the uniform numbers of five of their players. Three are Hall-of-Famers: Tony Gwynn (number 19), Dave Winfield (31), and Trevor Hoffman (51). The fourth was the franchise's first star player and a fan favorite, Cy Young Award-winner Randy Jones (35). The fifth? He played only four full seasons for the Padres. He accumulated 1.4 WAR in 605 games, batting .275 with 61 home runs, adding up to an OPS+ of exactly 100. He also hit the most important home run in franchise history.

Decades later, Steve Garvey's game-winning two-run home run in the bottom of the ninth inning against Lee Smith of the Chicago Cubs in Game Four of the 1984 National League Championship Series was ranked as the greatest sports moment in San Diego history.[1] For the game, Garvey had four run-scoring hits and five RBIs. Padres Manager Dick Williams called it the best single-game performance he had ever seen—this from the man who managed Carl Yastrzemski during his Triple Crown season in 1967 and the Oakland A's first two World Series winners in 1972 and '73.[2]

Garvey retired from baseball after an injury-filled 1987 season, and his uniform number (6) was retired by the Padres the very next April. Even years later, this surprises some baseball fans. Many remember Garvey as a Dodger—his best years were in Los Angeles, his tenure in San Diego was short, and his hitting statistics with the Padres were average.[3] But Garvey also helped elevate the franchise into a contender for the first time and his home run led the Padres to their first pennant. As Garvey said at the time, there's only one first. Of course, the Game Four win tied the best-of-five series at 2–2, so the Padres still had to win Game Five to make the home run truly iconic. They did.

Garvey played the first 14 seasons of his career for the rival Los Angeles Dodgers. He was the team's biggest star and the fan-favorite face of the franchise. After a few tours at third base and corner outfield, Garvey became the starting first baseman for the Dodgers in 1974. Later that summer he made his first of 10 All-Star teams and was named All-Star Game MVP.

At the end of the season, he added Gold Glove and National League MVP awards. From 1974 to 1981, Garvey made eight consecutive All-Star Game appearances and averaged 191 hits, 21 home runs and 99 RBIs, with a slash line of .309/.346/.474 and an average OPS+ of 128.

Garvey established a reputation as a clutch hitter and was even better in the playoffs. In 45 playoff games for the Dodgers, Garvey amassed a .346 batting average, hammered 10 home runs and drove in 22 runs, slugging .571 for an OPS of .942. Garvey and the Dodgers were models of consistency from 1974 to 1981, averaging 92 wins per full season and playing in four World Series, winning one. The infield of Garvey at first, Davey Lopes at second, Bill Russell at shortstop, and Ron Cey at third played more than eight seasons together—still a major league record. Following the Dodgers' victory over the Yankees in the 1981 World Series, Garvey was widely regarded as one of the premier players in baseball.

Meanwhile, down Interstate 5 in San Diego, the Padres were better known for their owner's fast-food restaurants (McDonald's), their mascot (the San Diego Chicken), and their taco-colored uniforms (brown and yellow) than their play on the field. Over their first 15 seasons (1969–83), the Padres had exactly one winning season, and they never finished higher than fourth place in the six-team NL West or closer than eight games behind the division winner. In the early seasons, more San Diegans were visiting the zoo and Sea World than the ball park.

Ray Kroc purchased the Padres in 1974 for $11 million to keep them in San Diego. Frustrated that the Padres had not become a winner on the field, Kroc promoted Jack McKeon to general manager in 1980. Trader Jack was the architect of the 1984 pennant winners. He reshaped the roster by trades, the amateur draft, and free agency. In his first trade, after the 1980 season, he engineered an 11-player deal that brought future All-Star catcher Terry Kennedy from the St. Louis Cardinals. In the 1981 amateur draft, he selected Gwynn in the third round. After the 1981 season, he made a six-player deal that sent Ozzie Smith to the Cardinals for shortstop Garry Templeton.

In 1982, Garvey earned $361,000 in the final season of a six-year, $1.9 million contract he'd signed with the Dodgers in 1977. Garvey had a disappointing season in 1982 on and off the field. He got off to a terrible start and sensed that the Dodgers did not really want him. His home life was in turmoil, and his marriage ended in a messy divorce. After the season he turned 34 and became a free agent. Dodgers fans could not imagine Garvey in another uniform, but the Dodgers' front office did not have a history of signing their own free agents. The team was starting to rebuild with younger prospects. The Dodgers reportedly offered Garvey $5 million for four years. Disillusioned by the club's business decision, Garvey didn't sign. McKeon was in the midst of his five-year plan to build a contender in San Diego, and he outbid several other teams. He signed Garvey for $6.6 million for five years.[4] While those salaries seem quaint now, it was one of the most lucrative deals at the time. Garvey's production had started to decline, but he'd still played in all 162 games for the Dodgers in 1982 (starting 154) and took his iron-man streak to San Diego.

Garvey tied, then broke, the National League record for consecutive games played in a rousing homecoming at Dodger Stadium in April 1983, but in July he broke his thumb in a home-plate collision as he tried to score on a wild pitch. The play ended his season and his consecutive-game streak at 1,207—still a National League record. The Padres finished 1983 with a second consecutive 81–81 record under irascible old-school manager Williams. In the offseason, Trader Jack and the Padres signed free-agent reliever Goose Gossage, 32, and acquired 39-year-old third baseman Graig Nettles in a trade, both escaping the Bronx Zoo for a fresh start. Gossage and Nettles were key members of the Yankees clubs that had faced Garvey and the Dodgers in some epic World Series.

Following these player moves, *Sports Illustrated* predicted in its 1984 season preview that the Padres could have a "whale of a season."[5] Prophetic—except the Padres had to compete with land animals in 1984: Cubs and Tigers. The Padres started the season 10–2, were tied for first place at the end of May, took over first place on June 9 for the rest of the season, and clinched their first West Division crown on September 20.

Along the way, Garvey carried the Olympic torch through San Diego in the lead up to the Los Angeles Games—organized by Peter Ueberroth, who replaced Bowie Kuhn as baseball commissioner during the

playoffs in October 1984. In August, the first-place Padres and second-place Atlanta Braves were involved in one of the worst "bean-brawl" games in major league history. The final tally included two bench-clearing brawls, multiple mini-brawls, over a dozen ejections and at least five fan arrests. Williams was suspended 10 games. Padres bench player Tim Flannery later called it a rallying point for the team. San Diego finished 92–70, 12 games ahead of the Braves. Gwynn, in his third year, batted .351 to capture the first of his eight batting average titles. Gossage finished 10–6 with a 2.90 ERA and 25 saves; he pitched 102 innings in a bygone era of multi-inning firemen. Garvey led the team with 86 RBIs.

In the East Division that season, the Cubs won 96 games and beat the New York Mets by 6½ games. The Cubs were led by their own third-year star, second baseman Ryne Sandberg, the eventual NL MVP and one of the best second baseman of the 1980s. Before the season started, the Cubs traded young players Carmelo Martinez and Craig Lefferts to the Padres— and both turned out to be major contributors in 1984. In May, in order to make room for Bob Dernier and Gary Mathews in the outfield, the Cubs traded Bill Buckner to the Boston Red Sox for Dennis Eckersley and kept Leon Durham at first base—a coincidental connection that would not reveal itself until after Durham's and Buckner's misplays in the 1984 NLCS and the 1986 World Series. Cey, Garvey's longtime Dodgers teammate, had been traded to the Cubs before the 1983 season. Cey recommended Rick Sutcliffe, a former Los Angeles teammate, to Cubs management. After he was acquired in a trade in June, Sutcliffe won 16 games and the NL Cy Young award.

The Padres and Cubs were the last two National League teams to make it to the League Championship Series, which began when division play started in 1969. They'd split 12 games during the 1984 regular season, but the Cubs were favored to win the series. The Cubs had 15 players with playoff experience—the Padres just five. The Cubs led the National League in runs scored, played in a stronger division, and had the majors' best record against good teams. The 1984 season was the last with a five-game LCS. Home field was still determined on a rotation system, with the first two games in the NL East park and the final three games in the NL West park. So the Cubs hosted the first two games at Wrigley Field.

ABC broadcast the NLCS with announcers Don Drysdale, Reggie Jackson, and Earl Weaver. Ernie Banks was named an honorary member of the 1984 Cubs and threw the ceremonial first pitch before Game One.

"Mr. Cub" saluted the crowd and threw the pitch into the ground 10 feet in front of the mound. It bounced straight to Cubs catcher Jody Davis—perhaps a good omen. Center fielder Dernier hit a lead-off home run against the Padres' ace, Eric Show. Four home runs later, including one by Sutcliffe that flew out of Wrigley Field, the Cubs had a shutout and the franchise's first postseason win since 1945. After taking Game Two by a score of 4–2, the Cubs had an 84 percent chance of winning the series and returning to the World Series against the Detroit Tigers—the team that beat the Cubs 4–3 in the 1945 World Series.[6]

Even though no National League club had ever come back from a 2–0 deficit in a five-game series, thousands of fans were waiting for the Padres players for a rally at Jack Murphy Stadium when the team arrived from the airport after the two losses in Chicago.[7] Before Game 3, the normally reticent Templeton got the crowd fired up by waving his cap during player introductions.[8] During the game, the stadium played "Cub-Busters," a parody of the theme song from the 1984 movie *Ghostbusters*. The fans donned Cub-Busters T-shirts and sang "We ain't 'fraid o' no Cubs." Second-year player Kevin McReynolds hit a home run and Ed Whitson pitched the Padres to a 7–1 win, the franchise's first playoff victory. After the Game Three win, Williams acknowledged the fans for rallying his club.[9] Whitson predicted if they could win Game Four they had a real shot at winning the series.[10]

Game Four, on Saturday, October 6, started at twilight on the West Coast. With two outs in the third inning, Garvey pulled a double down the left field line, scoring leadoff man Alan Wiggins from first for a 2–0 lead. After the Cubs took a 3–2 lead on homers by Davis and Durham, Garvey singled home the tying run in the fifth inning, again with two outs. In the seventh, with two outs and a runner on second base, the Cubs intentionally walked Gwynn to get to Garvey, who promptly lined a single to left field for another two-out RBI. Gwynn later scored to put the Padres ahead, 5–3.

The Padres brought in Gossage in the eighth inning to close out the game. In the regular season Gossage had gotten at least six outs in 28 of his 62 outings. But on this day, he surrendered three hits and two runs in the eighth to tie the game at 5–5. The Cubs called on their own closer, Smith, to pitch the bottom of the eighth. The Padres pinch-hit for Gossage and did not hit the ball out of the infield. In the top of the ninth, the Cubs loaded the bases off Lefferts but could not score. Smith was back on the mound to face the top of the Padres' lineup in the bottom of the ninth.

Although often thought of as a Los Angeles Dodger, Steve Garvey is remembered in San Diego as a Padre.

Wiggins, a prolific bunter, led off and bunted foul on strike three for the first out. In his second inning of work, Smith's fastball was still touching 99 mph. No problem for the league leader in batting average—Gwynn reached base on a line-drive single, bringing up Garvey, who was hitless in eight at-bats against Smith lifetime. He was looking for a pitch out over the plate. The first pitch was high and away for ball one. Garvey read the speed of the pitch. Smith threw to first to check on Gwynn. The next pitch to Garvey was a high fastball over the plate. Drysdale had the live call on ABC: "Deep right field, way back. Cotto going back to the wall. It's gone! Home Run Garvey! And there will be tomorrow!"

Garvey, normally undemonstrative, rounded the bases with his right arm raised, saluting the crowd and signifying victory. His delirious teammates met him at home plate. In his postgame interview with ABC, Garvey was asked by Tim McCarver how he came through every time—three two-out, run-scoring hits plus a game-winning home run. Garvey, in his typical understated style, said simply, "It was my pleasure." Later, Garvey was a little less modest, calling it one of his top two or three games.[11]

In the decisive Game Five Sunday afternoon in San Diego, the Cubs turned to Sutcliffe, their ace and the winner of Game One. The Cubs knocked Padres starter Show out of the game in the second inning and had a 3–0 lead through five, giving the Cubs an 88 percent win probability.[12] The Padres plated two runs in the sixth on sacrifice flies to make it 3–2.

In the seventh, the Padres bunted base runner Martinez—the tying run—to second. Padres reserve Flannery came up to pinch hit. As he stepped into the batter's box, he saw Cubs catcher Davis's shadow and knew he was setting up inside. Flannery looked for a first-pitch inside fastball and hit a sharp grounder to first base.[13] Drysdale had the call: "Groundball hit to Durham—right through his legs! Here comes Martinez. We're tied at three."

Before the inning ended, Wiggins singled, Gwynn doubled in two more runs, and Garvey singled in Gwynn. Gossage closed out the 6–3 win, and the Padres reached the World Series for the first time. Legendary Padres announcer Jerry Coleman had the call on the final out: "One hopper to Nettles. To Wiggins. And the Padres have the National League pennant! Oh, Doctor! You can hang a star on that baby!"

Of course, the Cubs did not return to the World Series against the Tigers. Leon Durham's error just added to the legend of Cubs postseason goats, ghosts, and other demons (not exorcised until their victory in the 2016 World Series). For the Padres, the comeback against the Cubs was the highlight of the season, as they fell to the heavily favored Tigers in five games in the World Series. Owner Ray Kroc had passed away in January 1984, and the team had dedicated the season to his memory. Interviewed before Game One of the World Series, his widow, Joan Kroc, said both teams were winners and she was sure Ray was smiling down.[14]

Garvey finished the NLCS batting .400 with seven RBIs and was named the series MVP. Although he played less than five full seasons for the Padres, his was the first number the club retired, signifying his outsized impact for the also-ran franchise. Gossage, who was on the mound for the final pitch of the 1984 NLCS and the decisive pitch of the World Series, captured the defining spirit of the moment. "To turn a city on for the first time like that, that was the most special part of the San Diego experience, to see the city turn upside-down when we beat the Cubs."[15]

In an interview years later, Bob Costas summed up Garvey's baseball legacy nicely: "Garvey is a guy who came up big in a lot of big moments—All-Star Games, World Series, and LCS. …I guess he will never be in the Hall of Fame, but in the prime of his career, he was a more significant player than some who are in Cooperstown."[16] Of his many big baseball moments, his Game Four home run remains the most iconic single moment in 50 seasons of Padres baseball. ■

Notes

1. Bryce Miller, "Garvey's Sweet Swing Delivers No. 1 Moment in San Diego Sports History," *San Diego Union-Tribune*, December 25, 2016.
2. Dick Williams interview on "MLB 1984 Baseball Greatest Hits—World Series Highlights," ESPN, October 6, 1985.
3. "Garvey's No. 6 Should Be Unretired," *San Diego Union-Tribune*, April 12, 2012; Jeff Sanders, "Friar talk: The Padres' Franchise Four," *San Diego Union-Tribune*, April 23, 2015. The Dodgers have not retired Garvey's number. Though it made an exception for the late Jim Gilliam, the team's policy is to only retire the jersey numbers of Hall of Fame players.
4. "Garvey Signs Padres Contract," *The New York Times*, December 22, 1982. "Garvey's a Padre: $6 Million Man," *San Diego Union-Tribune*, December 21, 1982.
5. Ivan Maisel, "Scouting Reports—San Diego Padres," *Sports Illustrated*, April 2, 1984.
6. Neil Paine, "The Cubs Curse is Now More Likely to End Than Continue," *FiveThirtyEight*, October 21, 2016.
7. Tim Flannery interview on "We Know Postseason—Tim Flannery Remembers Padres Victory," MLB Network, October 23, 2017.
8. Garry Templeton interview, Game Four pregame show, ABC, October 6, 1984. Although some player recollections include Templeton waving a towel, video shows it was his cap that he waved while firing up the crowd during player introductions.
9. Dick Williams interview, Game Four pregame show, KFMB-TV San Diego, October 6, 1984.
10. Ed Whitson interview, Game Four pregame show, KFMB-TV San Diego, October 6, 1984.
11. Steve Garvey interview on "MLB 1984 Baseball Greatest Hits."
12. Baseball-Reference.com.
13. Tim Flannery interview, MLB Network.
14. Joan Kroc interview World Series Game One pregame show, KNSD-TV San Diego, October 9, 1984.
15. Chris Jenkins, "Padres First World Series So Meaningful, *San Diego Union-Tribune*, October 20, 2014.
16. Bryce Miller, "San Diego Propels Garvey into All-Star Spotlight," *San Diego Union-Tribune*, July 7, 2016. Steve Garvey's highest vote total for the National Baseball Hall of Fame was 42 percent.

Tony Gwynn

Meeting Baseball's Best Hitter

Michael J. Schell

I don't like to compare myself to hitters of the past because people always start talking about eras— 'Gwynn's got to face four different pitchers in a game'—all that stuff. Forget all that. It's still the game of baseball. When I'm dead and gone, all that will be left is the numbers. They won't remember how much heart a person had, or how consistent he was, they'll just look at the numbers. And the numbers will tell you that I won eight batting titles; that I tied Honus Wagner for winning the most. The numbers will tell them that Wagner was a .345 lifetime hitter; and that I am a .340 lifetime hitter. So who was better? Honus Wagner. That's how it will be judged.

—Tony Gwynn[1]

"Gwynn will look at tapes for hours. He has one tape of each team. Each tape has all his at-bats against that team in the season. He has a tape…featuring all his at-bats in the previous season."

—George F. Will[2]

"Relative to the right wall of human limitation, Tony Gwynn and Wee Willie Keeler must stand in the same place—just a few inches from theoretical perfections (the best that human muscles and bones can do). But average play has so crept up upon Gwynn that he lacks the space for taking advantage of suboptimality in others."

—Stephen Jay Gould[3]

I met baseball's best hitter! No, not Babe Ruth, who died in 1948. He is baseball's best batter. No, not Ty Cobb, who died on my fourth birthday, in 1961. He is baseball's best "unadjusted" hitter. Not Honus Wagner (who actually had a .328 lifetime batting average). Not Ted Williams. Not even Wee Willie Keeler! To a sabermetrician like me, adjustments are important—nay, critical—to evaluating player performance. The moniker, "baseball's best hitter," properly belongs to Tony Gwynn.

First, I should explain that the term "best hitter" is a vague one. I define it to be "best at getting hits." The classic metric for this is batting average. Some baseball pundits prefer to say that batting average measures ability as a "pure hitter" rather than as a "hitter." OK, fine. Call Gwynn "baseball's best pure hitter." Why should we even care about this title, though? Aren't sabermetricians all about wins, wins, wins, which essentially comes from runs, runs, runs— so concepts like WAR (wins above replacement), OPS (on-base-plus-slugging), or linear weights become the metrics of choice? Well, this sabermetrician cares about more than wins. There is an art to hitting—baseball

swings can be beautiful. Just watch a regular-season game. A single typically gets much more applause than a walk. In Internet terms, it gets more "likes." Winning shouldn't be everything, otherwise a late-season game between two non-contenders should just be canceled.

Oh, I define "best batter" (or perhaps "best all-around batter") as the player with the best ability to produce runs (thus wins) in a given plate appearance, while "best player" is the best all-around player, which includes base running, fielding, and pitching abilities. Yes, Babe Ruth wins both of these awards.

Baseball-Reference.com shows Gwynn tied for 18th with Jesse Burkett and Nap Lajoie with a .3382 lifetime batting average in 18 seasons, all with the San Diego Padres.[4] Meanwhile, Cobb steals the top spot with a .3662 mark. In my 1999 book, *Baseball's All-Time Best Hitters*, I recommended that four adjustments be made to determine who really deserves to be called the "best hitter": for late-career declines; league average; player talent pool; and ball park.[5] The second and fourth adjustments are now a standard part of sabermetric adjustment, although there isn't consensus on how to most properly do so. The talent pool is a much

NATIONAL BASEBALL HALL OF FAME AND LIBRARY, COOPERSTOWN, NY

Tony Gwynn played his entire major league career for the Padres and was elected to the Hall of Fame on his first ballot.

more difficult adjustment to make, but the concern certainly pops up, especially when comparing players before and after integration in 1947. Some analysts identify a subset of years for a player as "prime years," a version of the first adjustment. I won't talk further of alternative adjustment methods, but simply apply what I think is the best analytic approach and report the results.

My adjustment for late-career declines uses only the first 8,000 at-bats of a player's career. That led me to fly from North Carolina in late July 1997 to San Diego to see Tony Gwynn's 8,000th at-bat. That week, Gwynn was on the cover of both *Sports Illustrated* and *The Sporting News*, as he was batting close to .400. *SI* had the provocative title "The Best Hitter Since Ted Williams," who intriguingly was a San Diego native and the second-"best hitter" behind Cobb, using a league average-type adjustment.[6] Notably, *SI* adopted the same definition as mine for "best hitter" and awarded Gwynn the sixth spot, using an obviously imperfect adjustment of the league average. It had two key imperfections: 1) the adjusting season aver-age combined data from both leagues, though AL pitchers have rarely batted since 1973, a transition that resulted in a seven-point jump in the league batting average—thereby hurting Gwynn by 3.5 points; and 2) the composite league average wasn't weighted by the player's at-bats for each of the seasons. Had *SI* done both properly, Gwynn would have slipped past Williams into second, also getting past Hornsby, Lajoie, and Keeler. I wanted to meet Gwynn and tell him that he was the best hitter in spite of Williams.

In *Baseball's All-Time Best Hitters'* adjusted world, Gwynn edged Cobb by a razor-thin margin of nine adjusted hits, a gap of .0011 batting-average points. The talent pool adjustment was based upon the standard deviation of "regular players," defined later. Having made improvements on this estimate, my second book,

Baseball's All-Time Best Sluggers (called *Best Sluggers* hereafter), concluded that Gwynn won by 22 adjusted hits.[7] The third-place hitter, Rod Carew, was six to eight points of average back in the books, effectively making it a two-man race. Today, we can improve the comparison of Gwynn vs. Cobb, as the ball park effects are better known. The ideal data to have are the home and road park batting data for all teams. While those were available for Gwynn when the books were written, only recently has Retrosheet had the park data for all but one of Cobb's seasons (1905–28).

ADJUSTMENT 1: LATE-CAREER DECLINES

Perhaps the most arbitrary adjustment is for late-career declines. I thought some milestone number was needed that was close to a full career for most players but would allow us to trim off some late years when most players' averages drop off; 8,000 AB was my choice then, and I still think it is a good one. In my view, identification of the "best hitter" shouldn't be affected by the player's wisdom in choosing his retirement date. Cobb gains about four points and Gwynn gains two by restricting batting average to 8,000 AB.[8] Gwynn became the 105th player to reach 8,000 ABs. Up through that time, only six players had higher lifetime batting averages than they did at 8,000 AB, with only one player being among the top 100 adjusted best hitters—Roberto Clemente. For such rare exceptions, I adopted the rule of using the superior average when it occurred, either at a higher milestone number of ABs or the full career. Neither Cobb nor Gwynn was an exception. At this first adjustment stage, Cobb is 243 hits ahead of Gwynn.

ADJUSTMENT 2: LEAGUE AVERAGE

This adjustment is extremely well-ingrained among sabermetricians. The adjustment calls for dividing the player's batting average by the league BA, either to obtain a "relative batting average," or to be reconstituted using a benchmark BA. I have scaled it to a .270 batting average, the typical BA for "regular" players in the NL in 1969–92, when the average league average was .255. "Regular players" are the players with the most plate appearances in the season, using a cutoff such that about 75 percent of the plate appearances are included. Thus, pitchers and most pinch hitters would be excluded. Note that some early sabermetri-cians mistakenly believed that the player's numbers should be removed from the league BA. All players are part of the league average, and in equally talented leagues with more teams, one should expect propor-tionally more great players; thus, it would be a bias to simply remove only the player of interest. This adjustment, while a quite powerful one, especially in adjusting the elevated average seen in the early live-ball era, say 1920–36, drops both Cobb's and Gwynn's averages only by a couple of points.

Table 1 shows the results after the four successive adjustments, the next two of which will now be described.

ADJUSTMENT 3: TALENT POOL

This adjustment, from a statistician's perspective, is simply a two-moment adjustment. Having obtained the batting average distribution for regular players (on a square-root scale, as this is more closely normally distributed), we are scaling the batting performance by the first two moments—the mean and the standard deviation. In my two books, I called this a "talent pool" adjustment, which it is. It is a powerful adjustment, especially for players in a newly established league. It is somewhat imperfect, however, as will be discussed further later. The concept is that when the standard deviation is larger, it shows a greater spread in the distribution of averages—because weaker players are getting significant ABs. In two well-known publications, Stephen Jay Gould highlighted the importance of this heterogeneity (spread captured by the standard deviation) as illustrative of weakness in an evolving system, such as baseball was in its early days.[9] Cobb played in a newly formed American League, joining the league in its fifth major-league season. Consequently, his average drops 25 points, and his hit lead narrows dramatically from 234 to 53.

ADJUSTMENT 4: PARK EFFECT

This is another well-ingrained adjustment among sabermetricians. The principal adjustment that is used is one based on run-scoring, contrasting runs scored by both teams in a given park compared with those obtained when the given park's home team plays on the road. It is better to adjust specifically for the event that one wants to adjust to rather than using the runs-based adjustment. My books described an adjustment, using home and road data for hits. Retrosheet now has park data back to 1906, so a more accurate park effect based on the exact data became possible for Cobb. The books had used an approximation method for Cobb's parks; overall, the approximation method had a Pearson correlation of 0.75 with the exact data when both were available.[10] The new results change the story rather dramatically. Navin Field, which Cobb played in from 1912 until 1926, which *Best Sluggers* had rated as giving Cobb an extra seven batting points per season, is actually a neutral park for hits. With the new, improved park data, Cobb wins by 5.2 hits rather than loses by 22!

Does that mean that I now believe Cobb is the best hitter? Well…according to the four-adjustment method laid out in my books, yes. However, the talent pool adjustment, which was applied as Adjustment 3, was also known to be imperfect. As noted in *Best Sluggers*: "The primary assumption that a 90th percentile player in say, 1901, would be a 90th percentile player today is not likely to be true for each offensive event."[11] It also assumes that an average player in 1901 is like an average player today as well—essentially by calculating the batting average distance to the average player scaled by the standard deviation. While the excess distance attained from the early years was shrunk to not excessively favor them, the average player from a newly formed league was not simultaneously determined to be worse. In summary, the talent pool adjustment used in step 3 substantially reduced, but did not eliminate, the advantage of playing in an inferior league.

Best Sluggers described nine steps in the development of an ideal adjustment system, with development to that time being to step 5—use of the batting average as a measure, with the four adjustments just described.[12] Step 6 was an "improved estimation of park effects," which was just reported above. Step 7 is a better assessment of the "changing ability of an 'average player' over history." Below, I present a partial movement forward on this step. Steps 8 and 9 are still beyond our current analysis.

A NEW AND IMPROVED TALENT POOL ADJUSTMENT

The standard deviation (SD) adjustment that comprised the third adjustment essentially equilibrates the players from all eras of play based on their percentile rankings in their seasons. While it did curtail the breakaway

Table 1. Batting Averages for Ty Cobb and Tony Gwynn after Successive Adjustments

Player	Raw BA	Raw BA to 8,000 AB	Mean-adjusted BA to 8,000 AB	Mean, SD-Adjusted BA to 8,000 AB	Mean, SD, Park-Adjusted BA to 8,000 AB	Mean, Park, Talent Pool-Adjusted BA to 8,000 AB
Cobb	.3662	.3701	.3670	.3422	.3402	.3376
Gwynn	.3382	.3398	.3377	.3356	.3396	.3396
Hit Gap	–	-243	-234.3	-52.7	-5.2	15.7

numbers of the superior players from weak talent pool seasons, it didn't further penalize them by considering the average player to be inferior. Table 2 shows the SDs for the first 25 AL major league seasons in five-year averages:

Table 2. Standard Deviations (SDs) of "Regular" Players in the American League in 5-Year Intervals

Years	SD
1901–05	.0322
1906–10	.0326
1911–15	.0362
1916–20	.0343
1921–25	.0300

It is highest for 1911–15. Does this mean that the AL got worse after the first decade, before subsequently improving? Actually, the increased SD coupled with our knowledge of the league provides evidence of an improving league, one that became more heterogeneous as more mediocre hitters were being replaced by better hitters. Who were these hitters? They included: Ty Cobb (first year as a regular player: 1906), Eddie Collins (1908), Frank Baker (1909), Tris Speaker (1909), and Shoeless Joe Jackson (1911). Notably, Cobb, Jackson, and Speaker all appear in *Best Sluggers* as adjusted top 10 "hitters." The improved adjustment is to apply the elevated average SD of the three highest years, 0.0363 (1911–13) to 1901–10 as well, as they represented lower talent pool seasons. The earlier seasons were likely worse; however, I don't yet know how to demonstrate that. I am asserting via revised talent pool adjustment that they weren't better. Two additional changes should be made as well: 1) when calculating a player's Z-score, rather than subtracting off the transformed mean from the season one should subtract off the standardized average (.5191 on the square-rooted scale), and 2) one should divide by the standardized SD, .0263, rather than the SD from the season whenever the player hits below average (this prevents elevation of subpar performances in a poorer talent pool season).

CONCLUSION

The new talent pool approach reduces Cobb's hit total by 20.8, from the seasons 1905–10. Thus, Cobb, with a .3376 average, finishes 15.7 hits behind Gwynn and his .3396 average. Further improvement of talent pool adjustment is needed; however, it would only further reduce Cobb's hits relative to Gwynn. As Cobb has already dropped below Gwynn in his adjusted hit total, we may conclude, albeit by the slimmest of margins (about a hit per season), that Tony Gwynn is the best hitter of all time![13]

Interestingly, *Best Sluggers* concluded that Tony Gwynn was also the best at not striking out. George Will certainly made a good choice of Tony Gwynn as the primary focus of the chapter "The Batter" in *Men at Work*.[14]

MEETING TONY GWYNN

I met Tony Gwynn, baseball's best hitter, on July 28, 1997, a couple of hours before he singled in his 8,000th career at-bat. He was very gracious. I gave him a copy of Gould's article "Entropic Homogeneity Isn't Why No One Hits .400 Any More" and briefly explained why the current *SI* article by Tom Verducci had not adjusted the batting averages well enough (data analysis came from the Elias Sports Bureau).[15] Gwynn, in turn, gave me a bat, one that he said "had hits on it"—and also hand-drawn racing stripes, which I think he must have done himself. What other player batting .391 in late July would give away one of his game bats? The day Gwynn died, I was called by Jay Caspian Kang of the *New Yorker*. I told Kang that the only way for Gwynn to be shown to be baseball's best hitter was through the adjusted batting average by a statistician, and that "I was his statistician."[16] I am honored that my name has been linked to Tony Gwynn's, who is baseball's best hitter.

Mr. Padre—we DO remember your heart and we don't just look at the raw numbers. ∎

Notes

1. Tony Gwynn, with Roger Vaughan, *The Art of Hitting* (New York: GT Publishing, 1998), dedication page.
2. George F. Will, *Men At Work* (New York: Macmillan, 1990), 221.
3. Stephen Jay Gould, *Full House: The Spread of Excellence From Plato to Darwin* (New York: Three Rivers Press, 1996), 114.
4. "Career Leaders & Records for Batting Average," Baseball-Reference, https://www.baseball-reference.com/leaders/batting_avg_career.shtml.
5. Michael J. Schell, *Baseball's All-Time Best Hitters* (Princeton: Princeton University Press, 1999).
6. Tom Verducci, "The Best Hitter Since Ted Williams," *Sports Illustrated*, July 27, 1997.
7. Schell, *Baseball's All-Time Best Sluggers* (Princeton: Princeton University Press, 2015).
8. Retrosheet data allowed me to get the hits totals exactly.
9. Gould, *Full House*; Gould, "Entropic Homogeneity Isn't Why No One Hits .400 Any More," *Discover*, August 1986.
10. Schell, *Baseball's All-Time Best Hitters*, 118.
11. Schell, *Baseball's All-Time Best Sluggers*, 214.
12. Schell, 212.
13. If one doesn't apply the late-career decline adjustment, Gwynn easily wins: .3374 to .3299.
14. Will, *Men At Work*.
15. Verducci, "The Best Hitter Since Ted Williams"; Gould, *Full House*; Gould, "Entropic Homogeneity Isn't Why No One Hits .400 Any More, *Discover*, August 1986, 60–66."
16. Jay Caspian Kang, "Tony Gwynn: An Appreciation," *New Yorker*, June 16, 2014. https://www.newyorker.com/sports/sporting-scene/tony-gwynn-an-appreciation.

Relief Pitching and the San Diego Padres

A Half-Century of Excellence

Wayne M. Towers, Ph.D.

While the San Diego Padres experienced only two World Series in the half-century after their 1969 founding, they did have a long and storied history of relief pitching: three Hall of Fame careers; a Rookie of the Year and a Cy Young Award winner; and the 2004 denouement of a tragic figure.

The first Padre inducted into the Hall of Fame was of course Tony Gwynn.[1] He was joined 11 years later by reliever Trevor Hoffman, whose "Trevor Time" with the Padres included 552 of his 601 career saves.[2] But Hoffman was only one of three Hall of Fame relievers who toiled for the Padres. He was preceded by both Rollie Fingers, who was with San Diego in 1977–80, and Rich Gossage, who pitched for the Padres in 1984–87.

After a five-save debut in 1993 (two of them with the Florida Marlins), Hoffman's sophomore log of 20 saves with the Padres would be his last season with fewer than 30 saves (with the exception of a 2003 injury year) until 2010, his final season.[3] This skein of 14 seasons of 30-plus saves included nine seasons with 40-plus saves and 53 saves in the 1998 National League pennant campaign. From 1993 through 2008, Hoffman saved 552 games for the Padres. He was the first relief pitcher with 500 saves, as well as the first with 600 (achieved while wearing a Milwaukee Brewers uniform). During his final season in 2010, he logged only 10 saves for the Brewers, ending his career with 601.

Despite his gaudy save numbers during the Qualcomm (previously Jack Murphy) Stadium years in park-like Mission Valley, Hoffman played a supporting role to Gwynn. He began to emerge from this relative obscurity beginning on July 25, 1998, to the resonant tolling of bells from the AC/DC song "Hells Bells," the brainchild of then-Padres-employee Chip Bowers. As Bowers tells it, "I just loved the irony of the song, given that we were playing in Mission Valley at the time and there was a mission directly beyond the outfield walls....To hear a mission bell ring prior to taking the mound, then you've got the Padres while talking about fire and brimstone and Hells Bells, I thought it was a great way to create some energy in the building. So, Hells Bells was born."[4]

Gwynn retired in 2001, leaving Hoffman to fill the role of star. At the new downtown Petco Park which opened in 2004, Hoffman took center stage. As "Hell's Bells" rang out, he reeled off four consecutive seasons of 40 or more saves (2004–2008). In 2018 he was inducted into the National Baseball Hall of Fame in Cooperstown wearing a Padres cap.[5]

Two other Hall of Famers also toiled in Mission Valley. Rollie Fingers (1968–85) was a Padres pitcher for four years (1977–80) while Rich Gossage (1972–94) also spent four years with the team (1984–87).

Rollie Fingers achieved baseball celebrity twice: first as a reliever with the 1970s Oakland A's teams that won five division titles and three World Series, then as the mighty warrior in the strike-altered 1981 baseball season who carried the Milwaukee Brewers to the American League East title, earning him both the Cy Young and MVP awards that year. Despite these baseball achievements, he is perhaps best known for his spectacular handlebar mustache, supposedly grown at A's owner Charlie Finley's behest.[6] Less celebrated than HOF Fingers's facial hair and his 341 career saves were the 108 he earned as a Padre (1977–80). His two best Padre years (37 saves in 1978 and 35 in 1977) were his career bests and both led all of MLB in individual season saves.[7] His impact on San Diego pitching was palpable. In 1976, the year before Fingers joined the club, they had 47 complete games and 18 saves. In 1977, his first year with the club, the Padres fell to six complete games, but rose to 44 saves, featuring 35 by Fingers.[8]

The third Hall of Fame reliever to toil in San Diego, Rich Gossage, made his presence felt by earning 83 of his 310 career saves in Mission Valley, and contributing notably to the 1984 pennant drive with 25 crucial saves.[9] As with Fingers, Gossage was better known for his earlier years with another team and for his formidable facial hair. As Gossage told many writers, "I didn't grow it to be intimidating...I grew it to tick off Steinbrenner."[10]

With George Steinbrenner's New York Yankees (1978–83), he registered 150 of his 310 career saves, and led the AL in saves in 1978 with 27 and MLB in 1980 with 33.[11] In San Diego, he reeled off three consecutive 20-plus saves seasons before stumbling to 11 saves in 1987. After San Diego, he spent 1988 through 1994 gathering 21 saves with six different teams.

We also have two notable Padres relievers who did not make the Hall of Fame, but who managed single season achievements with a 1976 Rookie of the Year and a 1989 Cy Young Award. Neither Butch Metzger nor Mark Davis ended up with distinguished MLB careers.

After an uninspiring initial year with the San Francisco Giants (10 games; no saves in 1974) and a few 1975 appearances with the Padres (4 games; no saves), Metzger suddenly found himself in the spotlight in 1976, finishing tied for ninth in MLB games saved and sharing the 1976 National League Rookie of the Year Award with Pat Zachry, then of the Cincinnati Reds.[12] Metzger's 16 saves that year ended up representing 70% of his 23 career saves.[13] When Fingers arrived the next year in 1977, Metzger was relegated to middle relief, and then traded to the St. Louis Cardinals where he earned seven saves before being released.[14] In 1978, Metzger pitched briefly for the New York Mets before he was released and his MLB career ended.[15]

The other singular award was a 1989 Cy Young Award accorded to Mark Davis (1980–97) for a league-leading 44-save season.[16] Davis quickly turned his newfound celebrity into cash, signing a $10 million contract with the Kansas City Royals.[17] His stay with the Royals (1990–92) and subsequent travels through four other teams (1992–97) produced an undistinguished won-loss record (11–19). He did a second tour with the Padres (1993–94) during which he notched the final four saves of his 96-save career.

Rod Beck (1991–2004) provides a sad denouement to our trip through a half-century of standout Padres relief pitching. Beck was beloved by San Francisco Giants fans for his 199 saves (1991–97)[18]—and by Chicago Cubs fans for a brief stay (1998–99), featuring 51 saves in 1998.[19] After spending time with the Boston Red Sox (1999–2001), he was out of MLB in 2002 while recovering from Tommy John surgery.[20]

Beck was known for his colorful, party-animal personality. As he once said, "I sure don't think of myself as a fat person, just someone who carries extra weight. I've never seen anyone on the DL [disabled list] with pulled fat."[21] Beck's lifestyle was on full display as he rehabbed in the minors:

> …Beck, on the comeback trail in 2003, parked his RV behind the center field fence at the Cubs' Triple-A facility in Des Moines, Iowa. He refused

Hall of Famer Trevor Hoffman recorded 350 of his 601 career saves while the Padres played in San Diego's Mission Valley and another 202 after the move to downtown Petco Park, many to the tune of AC/DC's "Hell's Bells."

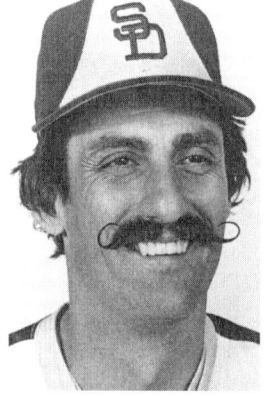

Although best known for his facial hair, Hall of Famer Rollie Fingers led MLB in individual season saves as a San Diego Padre in 1977 and 1978.

Rich "Goose" Gossage is well known for his years with the New York Yankees, but his 25 saves in 1984 helped the Padres to the National League pennant.

to check in to a hotel because that would mean admitting that he was really in the minors. The RV, of course, soon became the post-game hangout for players and fans, with Beck passing out the free beer.[22]

He found some redemption later in 2003, when the Padres signed him while Trevor Hoffman recovered from shoulder surgery.[23] Beck garnered 20 saves and became a San Diego fan favorite with "... his shoulder-length, wavy mullet, a long straggly mustache and a dangling [pitching] arm that ticked like a pendulum."[24] He remained with the Padres for his final baseball year in 2004, but earned no more saves in a back-up role, finishing with 286 career saves. His career with the Padres ended with a 2004 stint in substance abuse rehab.[25]

After being out of MLB for two years, Beck was found dead in 2007 at the age of 38, presumed not from his weight but from cocaine abuse.[26] His wife Stacey and even former teammates Hoffman and Scott Linebrink had staged interventions to try to get him back into rehab, in vain. Stacey was open about his death in the press: "The reason we're telling this story is so that other people will seek out the information, seek out the people who can help them. My daughter asked me to tell this story so that daddy doesn't die in vain without helping someone else."[27]

May the next 50 years bring relief pitchers as colorful and successful to San Diego as the first 50 years saw. ■

Notes

1. Gwynn, the "Mr. Padre" of San Diego's Mission Valley years (1969–2003), was inducted into Cooperstown in 2007.
2. Miguel Vazquez, "What 'Trevor Time' Meant to 2 Me," *East Village Times*, January 2018, https://eastvillagetimes.com/2018/01//what-trevor-time-meant-tome.
3. "Trevor Hoffman," Baseball Hall of Fame, https://baseballhall.org/hof/hoffman-trevor; Max Mannis, "Trevor Hoffman." SABR BioProject, https://sabr.org/bioproj/person/740006e2.
4. Bryce Miller, "Roots of Trevor Hoffman's 'Hell's Bells' stretch to one man's CD collection," *San Diego Union-Tribune*, January 31, 2018, https://www.sandiegouniontribune.com/sports/columnists/bryce-miller/sd-sp-millerhellsbells-20180131-story.html.
5. "Trevor Hoffman," [Hall of Fame biography].
6. Kevin Neary with Leigh A. Tobin, *Closer: Major League Players Reveal the Inside Pitch on Saving the Game*, Philadelphia: Running Press, 2013, 30; "Rollie Fingers," Baseball Hall of Fame; Voiss, "Rollie Fingers;" Zimniuch, *Fireman*, 85. As the story goes, Reggie Jackson, Oakland's star outfielder, showed up for spring training in 1972 with a mustache. His teammates did not like the idea…so they all started growing facial hair to protest.

Team owner Charles Finley, instead of making everyone shave, as the players hoped he would, offered a cash prize to the player who could grow the best facial hair by Opening Day. Finley felt the look would help sell tickets. Fingers grew a handlebar mustache that curled at the tips. It won the contest, and the mustache became his trademark look.
7. "Year-by-Year Top-Tens Saves," Date accessed January 31, 2015, https://www.baseball-reference.com/leaders/SV_top_ten.shtml.
8. John Thorn, *The Relief Pitcher: Baseball's New Hero* (New York: E.F. Duttion,1979), 181.
9. Zimniuch, *Fireman*, 98.
10. Jeff Miller, "Little Presence, Great Future." *Fort Lauderdale Sun-Sentinel*, March 30, 1997.
11. "Year-by-Year Top-Tens Saves," baseball-reference.com.
12. Retrosimba, "Why Padres Dealt NL top rookie Butch Metzger to Cards," Date accessed January 13, 2019, https://retrosimba.com/2017/05/15/whypadres-dealt-nl-top-rookie-butch-metzger-to-cards/.
13. David E. Skelton, "Butch Metzger," SABR BioProject, Date accessed January 8, 2019, https://sabr.org/bioproj/person/0c7eb75b.
14. Retrosimba, "Why Padres Dealt NL top rookie Butch Metzger to Cards."
15. Retrosimba, "Why Padres Dealt NL top rookie Butch Metzger to Cards."
16. James Clark, "Where Is the Love for Former Padres; LHP Mark Davis?" Date accessed January 19, 2019, https://eastvillagetimes.com/2018/03/where-isthe-love-for-former-padres-lhp-mark-davis.
17. Billy Brost, "Forgotten Friars: Mark Davis," Friars on Base, November 26, 2014, https://friarsonbase.com/2014/11/26/forgotten-friars-mark-davis.
18. Michael Saltzman, "San Francisco Giants Remembering 18 Darryl Hamilton and Rod Beck Today." Date accessed January 13, 2019, https://aroundthefoghorn.com/2017/08/05/ san-francisco-giants-remembering-darrylhamilton-rod-beck-today.
19. Jake Misener, "Chicago Cubs: Looking back at the career of Rod Beck," Date accessed January 13, 2019, https://cubbiescrib.com/2015/06/24/chicagocubs-looking-back-at-the-career-of-rod-beck.
20. Bloom, "Rod Beck Dead at 38—RIP Shooter."
21. Misener, "Chicago Cubs: Looking back at the career of Rod Beck.
22. Rick Chand, "When Rod Beck Ruled the World." Date accessed January 13, 2019, https://deadspin.com/271924/when-rod-beck-ruled-the-world.
23. Zimniuch, Fireman, 218.
24. Amy K. Nelson, "'Shooter' Beck lived as hard as he played," Date accessed January 13, 2019, http://www.espn.com/mlb/news/story?id=3060456.
25. Bloom, "Rod Beck Dead at 38—RIP Shooter."
26. "Ex-Reliever Rod Beck Dies at 38," *The New York Times*, June 28, 2007. Date accessed January 19, 2019, https://www.nytimes.com/2007/06/25/sports/baseball/25beck.html; Nelson, "'Shooter' Beck lived as hard as he played."
27. Nelson, "'Shooter' Beck lived as hard as he played."

The Silver Anniversary of Tony Gwynn's Quest for .400

Geoff Young

The 1994 players' strike deprived baseball fans of many simple pleasures. Among the casualties were postseason play, Matt Williams's assault on the single-season home-run record, and Tony Gwynn's pursuit of the hallowed .400 batting average—a feat not achieved since Ted Williams batted .406 in 1941.

The Padres entered the season, their 26th in the major leagues, still reeling from the previous year's fire sale orchestrated by owner Tom Werner.[1] With the glory of their inaugural World Series appearance in 1984 well behind them and the wounds of a 101-loss season still fresh in everyone's minds, expectations were minimal.

The Padres delivered on their lack of promise, finishing 47–70 in the abbreviated campaign thanks to the talent vacuum created by Werner.[2] Some youngsters acquired by general manager Randy Smith in the fire sale—Brad Ausmus, Derek Bell, Andy Ashby—flashed potential and gave hope for a brighter future, but for the most part, this was a team ill-equipped to compete and deserving of the worst record in the majors.

One bright spot for San Diego in 1994—perhaps the only bright spot—was Gwynn, who entered the campaign with a .329 batting average over 12 seasons, all with the Padres. He had won four National League batting titles and been an integral part of the 1984 team. As a nine-time All-Star with five Gold Glove awards and more than 2,000 hits under his belt, he had already compiled an impressive résumé.

After a few lackluster seasons (by his standards) as he entered his thirties, Gwynn rebounded with a .358 batting average in 1993. Dogged by chronic knee issues, he had been limited to 122 games, but entering his age-34 campaign, Gwynn looked to be as locked in as ever at the plate.

He came out of the gate strong, notching hits in each of his first six games. On April 23, at home against the Phillies, he went 5-for-5 with a double and a homer. The following afternoon he added three more hits, concluding a four-game multihit streak during which he went 13-for-17 against the Expos and Phillies.

Despite going 1-for-9 in the month's final two games, Gwynn ended April with a .395 batting average—impressive, but not too difficult to achieve in 76 at-bats, particularly for someone who once batted .370 over an entire season. Still, it was his highest showing for the month since he'd batted .434 a decade earlier in April 1984. Gwynn collected hits in 15 of the 18 games he played in and already had nine multihit games to his credit.

Gwynn started May just as he'd started April, collecting hits in each of his first six games. After three consecutive three-hit games May 11–14, his batting average stood at .419. An 11-game stretch during which he went 9-for-36 dropped Gwynn's batting average to .379, though four multihit games in the next six brought it back up to .393 at the end of the month.

Something else worth mentioning happened in May. On May 9, Gwynn's 34th birthday, he went hitless against the Reds. He did the same the following night. Then, on May 15, he went 0-for-3 against the Dodgers. The next night he repeated that performance against the Cubs. Those marked the only times he went hitless in consecutive games all season. Both came during a 13-game losing streak.

June brought more consistency from Gwynn, who had 14 multihit games in the 27 he played, batting .387 for the month. Highlights included a four-single game in a 3–1 victory at San Francisco on June 11 and a three-hit contest at home against the Dodgers on June 21. In the latter, Gwynn singled in the tying run in the bottom of the 13th inning and scored the game-winner.

June 21 also marked the beginning of a 10-game hitting streak, his longest of the season. Gwynn had two hits or more in eight of those games and brought his batting average back up from .378 (the last time it would fall below .380 all year) to .391 by month's end.

People were starting to notice. As Phillies batting coach Denis Menke told the *Philadelphia Tribune*, "If anyone can hit .400, in my opinion, it's Tony Gwynn. There are a lot of excellent hitters out there but I really can't think of anyone who has as good of a chance of doing it better than him."[3]

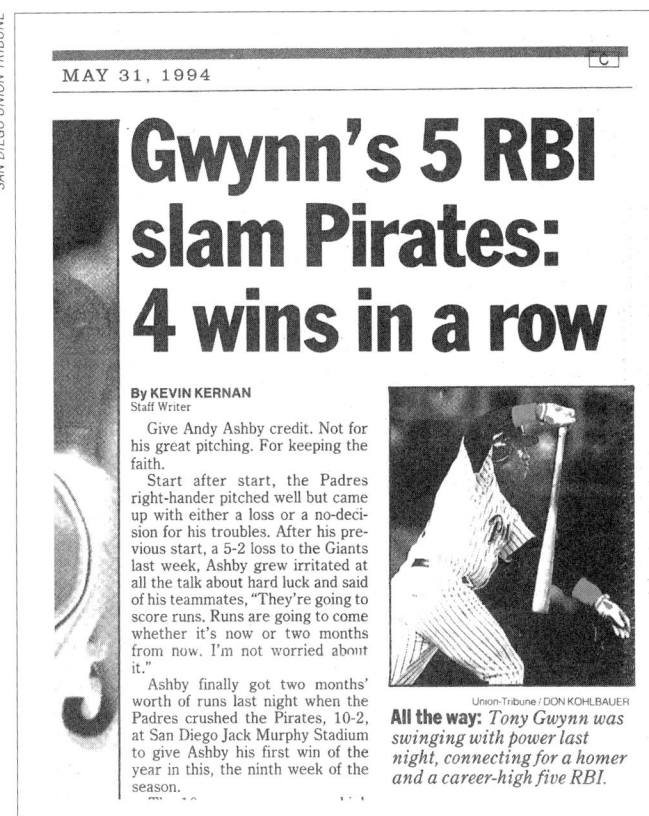

MAY 31, 1994

Gwynn's 5 RBI slam Pirates: 4 wins in a row

By KEVIN KERNAN
Staff Writer

Give Andy Ashby credit. Not for his great pitching. For keeping the faith.

Start after start, the Padres right-hander pitched well but came up with either a loss or a no-decision for his troubles. After his previous start, a 5-2 loss to the Giants last week, Ashby grew irritated at all the talk about hard luck and said of his teammates, "They're going to score runs. Runs are going to come whether it's now or two months from now. I'm not worried about it."

Ashby finally got two months' worth of runs last night when the Padres crushed the Pirates, 10-2, at San Diego Jack Murphy Stadium to give Ashby his first win of the year in this, the ninth week of the season.

Union-Tribune / DON KOHLBAUER

All the way: *Tony Gwynn was swinging with power last night, connecting for a homer and a career-high five RBI.*

Over the decades, few had seriously threatened to end the long drought since Williams had achieved the feat, and .400 was coming to be seen as a baseball unicorn. Rod Carew batted .388 in 1977, George Brett batted .390 in 1980, but nobody else had made a legitimate run at the mark. Gwynn downplayed his own chances, saying, "I'm too busy up there trying to hack" and "I know what type of hitter I am, so I never worry about .400. Talk to me in September. We'll see where I am then."[4,5]

Meanwhile, the threat of a work stoppage continued to grow stronger, casting Gwynn's words in a more ominous light. It was one thing to be chasing unicorns, but trying to avoid a seemingly inevitable strike was a different beast altogether. As he said, "I hope it doesn't happen, but my gut feeling is that it will, and anybody who's been around baseball for a long time feels the same way."[6]

Would Gwynn still be hitting well enough to seriously threaten .400 come September? Would he be playing baseball at all?

With such questions hanging over everyone's heads, Gwynn started July slowly, going 7-for-25 in his first eight games. He followed that with five straight multihit games, during which he went 12-for-23.[7] A few days later, he went 6-for-8 in a July 22 doubleheader at Philadelphia, raising his batting average to

.393. He finished with an 8-for-28 slide and ended up batting .370 for the month, his lowest mark for any month in 1994. Still, his season batting average stood at .385.

Despite his continued excellence, Gwynn remained unconvinced he could bat .400, though he did add an enticing caveat: "Sooner or later, somebody's going to do it. Realistically, I don't think I can do it. But the way things are going this year, who knows?"[8] Others held a different view. Former teammate Fred McGriff said, "Tony can hit .400 if anyone can."[9] Cincinnati Reds right-hander Jose Rijo agreed: "If he really wants to, yes, he can."

The next month promised to be a good test. When Carew made his run at .400 in 1977, he entered August batting .383 and batted "only" .363 for the month, dropping his season batting average to .378. When Brett made his run in 1980, he entered August batting .390 and proceeded to bat .430, raising his season batting average to .403. For Gwynn's part, he'd batted .448 in August a year earlier.

Gwynn seemed to enjoy the month again in 1994, starting it with three straight multihit games. After going 0-for-1 as a pinch-hitter on August 4, he went 12-for-27 over his next six games, the last of which proved to be the season finale. In that Thursday afternoon affair at Houston, he went 3-for-5, lifting his batting average to .394, the highest mark in baseball since Williams's .406 in 1941 and the highest in the National League since Bill Terry batted .401 in 1930.[10]

When comparing Gwynn's run with those of Brett and Carew before him, it's interesting to note just how consistent Gwynn was throughout the season. He did not experience the same ebbs and flows as his predecessors:

Batting Averages by Month

Month	Gwynn 1994	Brett 1980	Carew 1977
Mar/Apr	.395	.259	.356
May	.392	.329	.372
June	.387	.472	.486
July	.370	.494	.304
Aug.	.475	.430	.363
Sept./Oct.	NA	.324	.439

Brett entered June with a respectable but pedestrian .301 batting average and then batted a ridiculous .459 over the next three months before fading at the end. Carew essentially had a typical Carew season punctuated by two surreal months.[11] Gwynn, though, just hit and hit and hit.

Brett pushed his batting average from .267 to .406 from May 27 to August 30 thanks to a .469 batting average over 289 plate appearances. Carew had a similar streak from April 28 to July 1, when he batted .439 over 251 plate appearances. Gwynn's best streak pales in comparison: From June 10 to season's end he batted "only" .410 over 254 plate appearances. Unfortunately, the baseball world never got to see what could have been a very special final act, as the season came to an abrupt halt after the games of August 11.

A week before that, despite that scorching stretch, Gwynn continued to downplay his pursuit of history, saying, "Right now I don't even allow myself to think about it very much. If we get to September and I'm close then I'll take a shot at it. If not, I'm not going to worry."[12]

He also finally acknowledged what had become obvious to everyone else: "I honestly think I am a better hitter now than I've ever been. In terms of knowing what the pitchers are doing, what I'm capable of doing and then putting all the pieces together, I am definitely better. I am more mature and more patient. At the same time, I'm more aggressive and more under control."[13]

Still, Gwynn's run at .400 didn't seem to capture imaginations in quite the same way as Brett's and Carew's runs had. Part of this was due to the strike, but Gwynn's consistency may have also played a role. Where Brett's average remained above .400 into September and Carew's into July, Gwynn fell off in May and played catch-up the rest of the way.

Tony Gwynn waits for his pitch.

Batting Average Thresholds

	Gwynn	Brett	Carew
Last time	1994	1980	1977
Below .300	N/A	May 30	April 16
Below .320	April 20	June 3	April 17
Below .340	April 20	June 10	May 3
Below .360	April 21	July 13	May 14
Below .380	June 20	July 27	Sept. 13
At/above .400	May 15	Sept. 19	July 10

That being said, it's hard to muster much enthusiasm for a sport that cancels the final six weeks of its season because of labor issues. Then again, even before the work stoppage, the Padres were terrible, which couldn't have helped.[14]

Now, a quarter century later, we can reflect on what actually happened and speculate on what might have been. There are numerous ways to do the latter,

many of which will surely spark lively debate among dedicated fans and ultimately decide nothing (an agreeable diversion in its own right).[15] As for the former, poring over the numbers and quotations from that time is enough to satisfy, at least for a little while.

Gwynn didn't bat .400 in 1994, but he came as close as anyone has in the last 75 years. He won the National League batting title that year, as he did each of the following three seasons, batting .371 from 1994 to 1997.

Gwynn continued to play as long as his body would let him. He retired after the 2001 season, at age 41, with a .338 career batting average and 3,141 hits. He remains at or near the top of the leader board in almost every offensive category for the Padres.

After retiring, Gwynn became head coach of the San Diego State baseball team, where he remained until his untimely death from parotid cancer in 2014, at age 54. He was inducted into the Hall of Fame in 2007 and continued to be active in the community until his passing, forever cementing his legacy in San Diego. There is a Tony Gwynn Drive near Petco Park and a statue inside the park. The stadium at his alma mater bears his name.

Perhaps most fittingly, just a few miles northeast of the ballpark he called home for 20 years, the Tony Gwynn Memorial Freeway meets the Ted Williams Parkway. Gwynn couldn't quite catch his fellow San

Diegan in life, but now the two names come together in a daily reminder of their greatness. While passing the interchange during rush hour, it's hard not to think of the last man to bat .400 and the one to come closest since. ■

Notes

1. Dave Sheinin, "Fire Sale in San Diego Leaves Players, Fans Steaming," *Washington Post*, July 5, 1993.
2. Statistics and records throughout are from Baseball Reference.com, https://www.baseball-reference.com/.
3. Daryl Bell, "This could be the year for a record hitter," *Philadelphia Tribune*, June 24, 1994.
4. Paul Hagen, "Bear down, contenders: this could be stretch drive," *Philadelphia Daily News*, June 11, 1994.
5. Mike Burroughs, "Gwynn, teammates enjoying last laugh," *Colorado Springs Gazette-Telegraph*, June 28, 1994.
6. "Players say cap proposal likely will put lid on season," *St. Petersburg Times*, June 16, 1994.
7. Six if you count the All-Star Game, in which he went 2-for-5 and scored the winning run in the bottom of the 10th.
8. Jennifer Frey, "There's No Easy Out With Gwynn at Work," *The New York Times*, July 3, 1994.
9. Rod Beaton, "Gwynn punches away at hitting .400 for year," *USA Today*, July 12, 1994.
10. Shortly before his passing, Gwynn collaborated with San Diego brewery AleSmith on .394 Pale Ale to commemorate his 1994 season. It has become one of the more popular local beers and serves as an ongoing reminder of Gwynn's brush with .400, as does the Tony Gwynn museum now housed within AleSmith's headquarters.
11. To be fair, Carew sustained his efforts longer than Brett or Gwynn did. Carew came to the plate 694 times in 1977, versus 515 times for Brett in 1980 and 475 for Gwynn in 1994.
12. "Gwynning spirit: In the batter's box, Padre knows best," *Vancouver Province*, August 4, 1994.
13. *Vancouver Province*.
14. For what it's worth, Gwynn played in 45 of the Padres' 47 victories in 1994. In those games, he batted .511 (90-for-176). One is tempted to quip that if Gwynn wanted to hit .400, the Padres should have simply won more often.
15. For example, one might note that Gwynn had batted .434 (53-for-122) over the final two months of 1993. Gwynn also once batted .402 (251-for-624) over a 162-game stretch from July 27, 1993, to May 13, 1995. See "The year that Tony Gwynn hit .400," High Heat Stats, June 4, 2012. http://www.highheatstats.com/2012/06/the-year-that-tony-gwynn-hit-400/.

Contributors

MARK CAMPS is a former Giants beat writer and columnist for the *San Francisco Chronicle*. He is an honorary, lifetime member of BBWAA. After nearly 30 years as a sportswriter, he is now a senior communications consultant for a large health care organization.

ALAN COHEN serves as Vice President-Treasurer of the Connecticut Smoky Joe Wood Chapter, and is the datacaster for the Hartford Yard Goats, the Double-A affiliate of the Rockies. He has written 50 biographies for SABR's bio-project, has contributed to more than 40 baseball-related publications, and has expanded his research into the Hearst Sandlot Classic (1946–65), which launched the careers of 88 major-league players. He has four children and six grandchildren and resides in Connecticut with wife, Frances, and their cat, Morty, and their dog, Buddy.

ROBERT K. FITTS is the founder of SABR's Asian Baseball Research Committee, Rob Fitts writes about the history of Japanese baseball and the game's role in U.S.-Japan relations. He has published four books on the topic including *Banzai Babe Ruth* (winner of the 2012 Seymour Award) and *Remembering Japanese Baseball* (winner of the 2005 SABR Research Award). His next book on the history of early Japanese American baseball will be published by the University of Nebraska Press in 2020.

GORDON J. GATTIE is an engineer for the US Navy. His baseball research interests include ballparks, historical records, and statistical analysis. A SABR member since 1998, Gordon earned his PhD. from SUNY Buffalo, where he used baseball to investigate judgment performance in complex dynamic environments. Ever the optimist, Gordon dreams of a Cleveland Indians-Washington Nationals World Series matchup. Lisa, his wonderful wife who also enjoys baseball, continues to challenge him by supporting the Yankees. Gordon has contributed to multiple SABR publications and the Games Project.

STEVEN M. GLASSMAN's article, "Padres' Near No-Hitters," will be his fifth SABR convention article. He previously wrote "Philadelphia's Other Hall of Famers" (SABR43), "The Game That Was Not—Philadelphia Phillies at Chicago Cubs" (August 8, 1988, SABR45), "Walking it Off " (Marlins Postseason Walk-Offs, SABR46), and "A Hall of Fame Cup of Coffee in New York" (SABR47).

LESLIE HEAPHY is an Associate Professor of History at Kent state University at Stark and has written or edited six books and numerous articles on the Negro Leagues, women's baseball, and the New York Mets.

BILL LAMB is a retired state/county prosecutor. He is the editor of *The Inside Game*, the quarterly newsletter of SABR's Deadball Era Committee, and the author of *Black Sox in the Courtroom: The Grand Jury, Criminal Trial and Civil Litigation* (Jefferson, North Carolina: McFarland, 2013).

TOM LARWIN is a retired transportation engineer and heads up the San Diego Ted Williams SABR Chapter. He was a co-author of the book entitled *San Diego's First Padres* and *"The Kid": The Story of the Remarkable 1936 San Diego Padres and Ted Williams' Professional Baseball Debut* (2019).

KEVIN MILLS is a new member of SABR since 2018 and this is his first article for *The National Pastime*. During Kevin's Little League days, he became a fan of Steve Garvey and watched Game 4 of the NLCS at home on a black-and-white television during his senior year of high school. As a young baseball fan, Kevin collected baseball cards with his brother and recently rediscovered his Steve Garvey Topps rookie card (1971). Kevin is a lawyer in Washington, DC, and has had the opportunity to represent ownership groups in bids to purchase MLB franchises and media rights.

BILL NOWLIN has written seven books about Ted Williams, the most recent being *Ted Williams: First Latino in the Baseball Hall of Fame*. His eighth, *Ted & Jimmy*, will be about Ted Williams's work in raising money to fight cancer in children. He is a long-serving member of SABR's Board of Directors.

JOHN RACANELLI is a Chicago lawyer with an insatiable interest in baseball-related litigation. When not rooting for his beloved Cubs (or working), he is probably reading a baseball book or blog, planning his next baseball trip, or enjoying downtime with his wife and family. He is probably the world's foremost photographer of triple peanuts found at ballgames and likes to think he has one of the most complete collections of vintage handheld electronic baseball games known to exist. John is a member of the Emil Rothe (Chicago) Chapter of SABR.

FRED O. RODGERS is retired and living in Houston, Texas. He is the former President of the San Diego Ted Williams SABR Chapter in its formative years in the early 1990s and head of SABR 23 in San Diego in 1994. He started *Baseball Gold*, the San Diego Padres newspaper, with Kurt Bevacqua in October of 1982 and was the editor until June 1986. Fred now runs the baseballgold.com website. He was researcher for *The Stan Musial Scrapbook* published by *The Sporting News* in 1993. He is currently the owner of one of the largest collections of *The Sporting News* in the country.

GARY SARNOFF is an active SABR member who has attended 14 of the last 15 SABR conventions. He serves as chairman of SABR's Ron Gabriel Award Committee, which annually awards the author(s) of the best research, published or unpublished, about the subject of the Brooklyn Dodgers. He has contributed to SABR's Baseball Biography Project and the Jerry Malloy Conference. He has authored two books: *The Wrecking Crew of '33: The Washington Senators' Last Pennant* and *The First Yankees Dynasty: Babe Ruth, Miller Huggins and the Bronx Bombers of the 1920s*. He resides in Alexandria, Virginia.

MICHAEL J. SCHELL has been a SABR member since 1998, is a Senior Member in the Biostatistics and Bioinformatics Department at the Moffitt Cancer Center in Tampa, Florida. His two books, *Baseball's All-Time Best Hitters* (1999) and *Baseball's All-Time Best Sluggers* (2005), adjust player statistical data for era of play, talent pool, ballpark, and career longevity. His most provocative conclusion is that Tony Gwynn is the "best hitter" in baseball history.

MARK SOUDER served as the US Congressman for northeastern Indiana 1995–2010. He was a senior staff member in the US House and Senate for a decade prior to being elected to Congress. He was one of the primary leaders of the hearings on steroid abuse in baseball. He has previously contributed articles to *The National Pastime* in Chicago, New York, and Pittsburgh. He has also contributed to three previous SABR books and two upcoming SABR books on the San Diego Padres and the Boston Beaneaters. He is retired and lives in Fort Waync with his wife and his books.

WAYNE M. TOWERS, PhD is a retired SeaWorld San Diego educator and a retired college professor. Prior to retiring, he also worked as a data analyst for the *Oklahoman* and *Times* daily newspapers and for multiple business research firms. His published work includes "World Series Coverage in the 1920s" (Journalism Monographs).

TOM WILLMAN is a retired newspaper writer. Previous articles have appeared in *Northern California Baseball History*, for SABR's 1998 National Convention, and in *The National Pastime* for 2011, on baseball in Southern California.

BRIAN P. WOOD (WOODIE) is a long time San Francisco Giants fan and resides in Pacific Grove, California, with his wife Terrise. They have three sons—Daniel, Jack, and Nathan—and a dog, Bochy. A retired US Navy Commander and F-14 Tomcat Naval Flight Officer, Woodie is a Research Associate on the faculty at the Naval Postgraduate School in Monterey specializing in Field Experimentation of new technologies before they are sent to military forces.

FRED WORTH is the author of *College Mathematics Through Baseball* and a member of SABR's Biographical Research Committee. He has been a SABR member since 2001 and is a lifelong New York Mets fan

GEOFF YOUNG founded Ducksnorts, one of the world's first baseball blogs, in 1997. He penned regular columns at *The Hardball Times* from 2007 to 2011 and at *Baseball Prospectus* from 2011 to 2013. He is a co-author of *Baseball Prospectus* annuals 2012–2016, a co-editor of *Baseball Prospectus 2018*, and a contributor to several other baseball books.

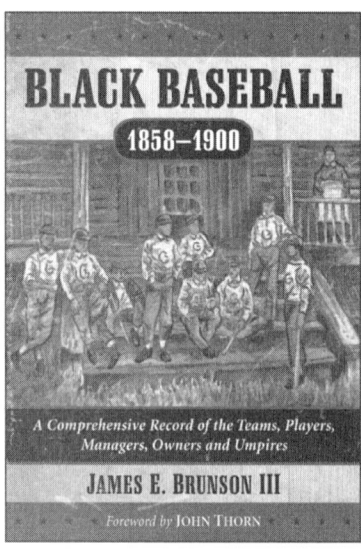

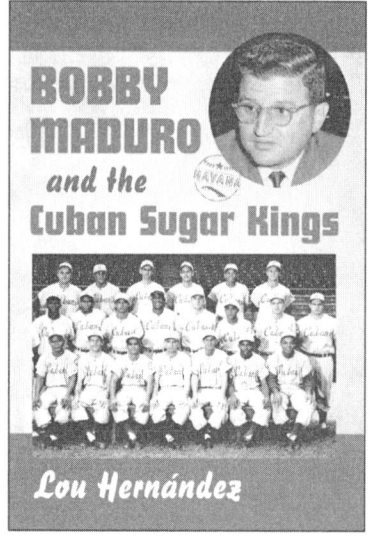